Effective Action
Research

Also available from Continuum

Developing a Questionnaire, Bill Gillham
Questionnaire Design, Interviewing and Attitude Measurement,
  A. N. Oppenheim

Effective Action Research

Research

2nd edition

Developing Reflective Thinking and Practice

Patrick J. M. Costello

Companion website
A companion website to accompany this book is available online at:
http://education.costello.continuumbooks.com

Please visit the link and register with us to receive your password and access to the
Companion Website.

If you experience any problems accessing the Companion Website, please contact
Continuum at info@continuumbooks.com.

continuum

Continuum International Publishing Group

The Tower Building   80 Maiden Lane
11 York Road   Suite 704
London SE1 7NX   New York, NY 10038

www.continuumbooks.com

British Library Cataloguing-in-Publication Data
A catalogue record for this book is available from the British Library.

ISBN: 978-1-4411-6375-2 (paperback)
       978-1-4411-3326-7 (hardcover)

Library of Congress Cataloging-in-Publication Data
Costello, Patrick J. M., 1959–
Effective action research: developing reflective thinking and practice /
Patrick Costello.
    p. cm.
Includes bibliographical references and index.
ISBN 978-1-4411-6375-2 (pbk.)
1. Action research in education. I. Title.

LB1028.24.C69 2011
370.72–dc22

                                      2010020557

Typeset by Newgen Imaging Systems Pvt Ltd, Chennai, India
Printed and bound in India by Replika Press Pvt Ltd

This book is for my son, Thomas Rónan Costello.

Contents

List of Illustrations   ix
Acknowledgements   x

Introduction   1

1 What is Action Research?   **3**
The nature of action research   3
Models of action research   8

2 Why Undertake Action Research?   **15**
The teacher as reflective practitioner   16
Relationships between educational theory and practice   17
The teacher as researcher   20
Teaching as a research-based profession   21
Problems with educational research   21
Teacher research and school improvement   23
Research and teachers' continuing professional development   24
The importance of action research   28

3 How Do I Develop an Action Research Project?   **31**
Choosing a research topic   31
Developing a research proposal   32
Undertaking a literature search and review   33
Working with your tutor   35
Undertaking action research projects: some preliminary considerations   42

4 How Do I Collect Action Research Data?   **45**
Collecting action research data: some preliminary considerations   45
Rigour in action research   52
Examples of action research projects   57

5 How Do I Analyse Action Research Data?   **65**
Analysing research data   66
A model of action research revisited   73
Concluding comments   77

6 How Do I Produce an Action Research Report?   **79**
Requirements and guidelines for writing action research reports   79

7 How Will My Action Research Report be Assessed?   **87**
A model of assessing progress in argument in higher education   88
Students' views of assessment   91
Assessing research projects: some examples   93

8 How Do I Publish My Action Research Report?   **101**
Students' experiences of writing for publication   101
Publishing action research reports in journals   104
Publishing action research reports through presenting conference papers   105

9 Recommended Further Reading   **113**
The importance of reading widely   113
Recommended further reading   114

10 Endnote: The Theory and Practice of Action Research   **117**
Rationale for the format of this book   117
Developing reflective thinking and practice   118

Bibliography   **121**
Index   **129**

List of Illustrations

Chapter 1
Figure 1.1 A basic action research model.   8
Figure 1.2 An extended action research model.   9
Figure 1.3 A representation of Denscombe's action research model.   12

Chapter 4
Figure 4.1 An ethical approval form preliminary checklist.   48
Figure 4.2 Details of your research project.   49
Figure 4.3 Research project information sheet.   50
Figure 4.4 Research project consent form.   51

Chapter 5
Figure 5.1 Observation chart.   67
Figure 5.2 Questionnaire.   69
Figure 5.3 Observation chart 1.   74
Figure 5.4 Observation chart 2.   75
Figure 5.5 A model of argument.   76

Chapter 6
Figure 6.1 Format for an undergraduate / postgraduate
research project report.   80
Figure 6.2 Format for a funded research project report.   81

Chapter 7
Figure 7.1 A model of assessing progress in argument in
higher education.   89
Figure 7.2 Questionnaire for students in higher education.   91

Chapter 8
Figure 8.1 Questionnaire.   102
Figure 8.2 Proposal to present a paper at a national conference.   106
Figure 8.3 Proposal to present a paper at an international
conference.   107
Figure 8.4 PowerPoint presentation.   108

Acknowledgements

I should like to thank the following:

- Alison Clark and Christina Garbutt, Commissioning Editors at Continuum, for their kind invitation to write this book.
- Dr. Donald Costello for the many discussions we have had about the theory and practice of action research.
- Glyndŵr University Wrexham for the award of a Research Fellowship, which enabled me to undertake desk-based research to underpin the arguments presented here.
- The College of Teachers for permission to draw on some of the research published in my paper 'Can we teach students in higher education to think critically?' (*Education Today*, Vol. 59, No. 1, 2009, pp. 20–25).
- Professor Rob Norris, formerly Dean of the Faculty of Arts and Education, North East Wales Institute of Higher Education, on whose assessment of an undergraduate examination paper the schema outlined in Figure 7.1 is based.

Since 1986, I have had the opportunity to test and improve my thinking about many of the key ideas presented in this book. With this in mind, I am very grateful to those teachers and student teachers with whom I have worked, at the University of Hull, Glyndŵr University Wrexham, and on behalf of the General Teaching Council for Wales, to develop a broad range of action research projects.

Introduction

The central aims of this book are to enable practitioners (students, teachers or researchers) to undertake effective action research and to offer an account of an action research project. The volume is divided into ten chapters, the first eight of which are headed by a commonly-asked question. Having examined the nature of action research and arguments for undertaking it in educational settings, I shall focus on developing an appropriate project, data collection and analysis, and producing, assessing and publishing action research reports. Chapter 9 provides suggestions for further reading and I conclude by offering a rationale for the format I have chosen to adopt in writing the book.

This volume is based on an earlier work, *Action Research* (Costello, 2003). I welcomed the invitation to update and expand on what I had written previously, as well as to add new chapters, not least because of the growing popularity of action research, which is currently very much in vogue. As is evident from the number of books and other publications that have been written on it in recent years (see Dick, 2004, 2006, 2009 and Chapter 9), many educators and other professionals have been adopting action research as their preferred mode of enquiry in a broad range of contexts. While the book is aimed primarily at practitioners undertaking a broad range of Education courses, it may also be used as a generic text for those undertaking action research projects in other disciplines. For example, a Google search of 'Action Research, Costello' reveals that the earlier volume has been referred to by researchers in the fields of, *inter alia*: archaeology, engineering, management, agriculture, public relations, music therapy, and cultural studies.

Encouraging students to think critically is one of the central objectives of higher education (Judge *et al.*, 2009; Moon, 2005). Linked to this is a concern, expressed by lecturers across a broad range of academic disciplines, that students should learn how to develop and present arguments (Costello, 2007b, 2009a). Indeed, whether you are participating in a group discussion, writing an essay or undertaking a research project, your ability to employ argument and to evaluate the arguments of others will generally be an important measure of achievement. Given this, the development of critical thinking, reasoning and argument skills in higher education is crucial. Frequently, these skills are taught through study skills programmes (Burke *et al.*, 2005; Durkin and Main, 2002; Goldfinch and Hughes, 2007), and/or research methodology seminars. A key theme of this book is to enable you to enhance such skills.

My main emphasis here will be on undertaking *effective* action research in the context of developing your reflective thinking and practice (Bolton, 2005; Hedberg, 2009). By 'effective' action research, I mean research that is undertaken with a specific aim or aims, that is conducted rigorously, using a variety of methods for collecting data, and that is reported accurately and fully, with appropriate conclusions and recommendations for future practice being offered. As we shall see in Chapter 1, action research involves a close relationship between reflection and action. Therefore, I shall focus throughout the book on reflective thinking as a means to underpin practice (Pollard, 2002; Pollard *et al.*, 2008; Taggart and Wilson, 2005). To this end, I have devised a series of 'Reflective Thinking Exercises' for you to consider as you work your way through the chapters. These exercises are intended to help you to develop your own action research project and to complete it successfully. I have also referred to some of my own research projects, in order both to illustrate key themes and to offer additional examples of collecting and presenting research data.

What is Action Research?

Chapter Outline

The nature of action research   3

Models of action research   8

My aim in this chapter is to offer an answer to the question 'What is action research?' In order to do this, I shall focus on two key themes:

- the nature of action research;
- the models of action research.

The nature of action research

In order to undertake an action research project within educational settings, we need to begin by giving some thought to the question: 'What is action research?' This, in turn, raises two further questions: 'What is research?' and 'What is educational research?' How are we to respond to these questions? One effective way of doing so is to place them in order, beginning with the most general, and then to do some reading and thinking about each in turn:

- What is research?
- What is educational research?
- What is action research?

4 Effective Action Research

Of the three questions, the most general is: 'What is research?' As a starting point, it is useful to examine some texts that discuss a broad range of approaches to engaging in research. These reveal that there are: (1) many different types of research; (2) numerous views as to the nature of each, how it should be conducted and what it aims to achieve.

For example, when discussing social research, Robson (2002, p. 26) cites the following: 'ethnography, quantitative behavioural science, phenomenology, action research, hermeneutics, evaluation research, feminist research, critical social science, historical-comparative research, and theoretical research'. It is useful to compare this list with some examples offered by Blaxter *et al.* (2001, p. 5): 'pure, applied and strategic research; descriptive, explanatory and evaluation research . . . exploratory, testing-out and problem-solving research; covert, adversarial and collaborative research; basic, applied, instrumental and action research.'

When reading general texts, you will see many references to these (and other) kinds of research. At this stage, it is important to note several points. First of all, do not be confused or distracted by the 'labels' that are attached to various kinds of research. Instead, ask yourself:

- What sorts of practices are being engaged in by those who undertake action research, ethnography, evaluation research etc.?
- What rationale is offered to support these practices?

In looking for commonalities between the types of research they cite, Blaxter *et al.* (2001, p. 5) offer a succinct summary: 'the basic characteristics shared by all of these . . . are that they are, or aim to be, planned, cautious, systematic and reliable ways of finding out or deepening understanding'.

Second, look for references to the particular kinds of research in which you are interested. For our purposes, both of the above lists are useful because they include 'action research'. Third, before moving on to examine more substantial accounts of action research, read and think carefully about the briefer outlines given by writers such as those cited above. Then ask yourself key questions:

- What do these outlines have in common?
- What is distinctive (if anything) about each?

Having considered the question 'What is research?' which he defines as 'systematic, critical and self-critical enquiry which aims to contribute to the advancement of knowledge and wisdom', Bassey (1999, p. 38) moves on to offer a response to the question, 'What is educational research?' Such research, he argues, 'is critical enquiry aimed at informing educational judgements and decisions in order to improve educational action' (p. 39). I shall return to the idea of 'critical enquiry' in Chapter 2. In the meantime, Bassey's definition, focusing as it does on the improvement of educational action, leads us to the third question 'What is action research?'

In order to answer this question, we will consider some definitions:

'Action research is a process of systematic reflection, enquiry and action carried out by individuals about their own professional practices' (Frost, 2002, p. 25).

'Action research is a term used to describe professionals studying their own practice in order to improve it' (GTCW, 2002b, p. 15).

'Educational action research is an enquiry which is carried out in order to understand, to evaluate and then to change, in order to improve some educational practice' (Bassey, 1998, p. 93).

'Action research combines a substantive act with a research procedure; it is action disciplined by enquiry, a personal attempt at understanding while engaged in a process of improvement and reform' (Hopkins, 2008, p. 47).

'Action research . . . is applied research, carried out by practitioners who have themselves identified a need for change or improvement' (Bell, 2005, p. 8).

'When applied to teaching, [action research] involves gathering and interpreting data to better understand an aspect of teaching and learning and applying the outcomes to improve practice' (GTCW, 2002b, p. 15).

'Action research is a flexible spiral process which allows action (change, improvement) and research (understanding, knowledge) to be achieved at the same time' (Dick, 2002).

'Action research is . . . usually described as cyclic, with action and critical reflection taking place in turn. The reflection is used to review the previous action and plan the next one' (Dick, 1997).

'[Action research] is an approach or an umbrella term, which . . . has proved to be attractive to educators . . . because of its emphasis on practice and problem-solving over a particular period of time' (Burgess et al., 2006, p. 60).

'[Action research] is both a sequence of events and an approach to problem solving' Coghlan and Brannick, 2005, p. 4).

'Action research is intended to combine a strong and rigorous research activity with a respect for participants' knowledge and understanding. It therefore brings together theory and practical knowledge, to test each other with the purpose of developing practice' (Coleman, 2007, pp. 484–85).

Considering a variety of sources in this way enables us to develop an understanding of action research and its central aims. Before we explore these areas further, please consider Reflective Thinking Exercise 1.1.

Reflective Thinking Exercise 1.1

1. Examine the above definitions of 'action research'.
2. Identify commonalities and differences in the definitions.
3. Write out your own response to the question: 'What is action research?'

This is an exercise I have given both to undergraduate and postgraduate students. Results usually demonstrate a substantial amount of agreement. Below, I outline the ten quotations once again, together with the responses typically made by practitioners. I have indicated each new idea in bold letters and underlined aspects covered by previous definitions. In this way, it is possible to see quickly both areas of agreement and difference:

'Action research is a **process of systematic reflection, enquiry and action** carried out by **individuals** about their **own professional practice**'.

'Action research is a **term** used to describe **professionals** studying their *own practice* in order to **improve** it'.

'Educational action research is an **enquiry** which is **carried out in order to understand, to evaluate and then to change**, in order to *improve some educational practice*'.

'Action research **combines a substantive act with a research procedure**; it is action disciplined by enquiry, *a personal attempt at understanding* while engaged in *a process of improvement* and **reform**'.

'Action research . . . is **applied research**, carried out by **practitioners** who have themselves identified a need for *change or improvement*'.

'When applied to teaching, [action research] **involves gathering and interpreting data** to better *understand* **an aspect of teaching and learning** and **applying the outcomes** to *improve practice*'.

'Action research is a **flexible spiral** *process* which allows *action (change, improvement) and research (understanding, knowledge)* to be achieved at the same time'.

'Action research is . . . usually described as **cyclic**, with *action* and **critical reflection** taking place in turn. The reflection is used to **review the previous action and plan the next one**'.

'[Action research] is an **approach** or an **umbrella term**, which . . . has proved to be attractive to **educators** . . . because of its emphasis on *practice* and **problem-solving** over a particular period of time'.

'[Action research] is both a **sequence of events** and an *approach to problem solving*.

'Action research is intended to combine a strong and **rigorous research activity** with a **respect for participants' knowledge and understanding**. It therefore **brings together theory and practical knowledge**, to test each other with the purpose of *developing practice*'.

An examination of these definitions suggests the following:

- Action research is referred to variously as a term, process, enquiry, approach, umbrella term, sequence of events, flexible spiral process, activity, and as cyclic.
- It has a practice-oriented, problem solving emphasis.
- It is carried out by individuals, professionals, practitioners and educators.
- It involves being respectful of participants' knowledge and understanding.
- It brings together theory and practical knowledge.
- It involves rigorous applied research, systematic, critical reflection and action.
- It aims to improve educational practice.
- Action is undertaken to understand, evaluate and change.
- Research involves gathering and interpreting (or analysing) data, often on an aspect of teaching and learning.
- Critical reflection involves reviewing actions undertaken and planning future actions.

Reading a number of accounts of action research is instructive because, in doing so, it becomes clear that there is both agreement and disagreement among authors as to what are its defining characteristics. For example, Denscombe (2007, p.123) suggests four such characteristics:

1. its practical nature;
2. its focus on change;
3. the involvement of a cyclical process;
4. its concern with participation:

   'Practitioners are the crucial people in the research process. Their participation is active, not passive'. However, Dick (2000) rejects the view that action research 'must be participative, or qualitative, or published. It often is and I accept this . . . But . . . I regard its cyclical/spiral process and its pursuit of both action and research as its defining characteristics'.

What are the consequences of such agreements and disagreements for the researcher? I would like to make two points here. First, if you are undertaking an action research project, it is important to understand, as I indicated in the Introduction, that the nature of such work is the subject of keen debate. As we have seen, writers offer their own competing and complementary views as to the fundamental character of action research. Second, if you are completing this project as part of a course of study for an academic qualification, you will need to engage critically with some of the arguments, positions and theoretical perspectives advanced by writers such as those mentioned above. I shall say more about this in Chapters 3 and 4.

Models of action research

In order to illustrate their views, many authors offer diagrammatic representations of action research models (see, for example, Coghlan and Brannick, 2005, pp. 21–25; MacNaughton and Hughes, 2009, pp. 1–3; Mertler, 2009, pp. 13–19). As Drummond and Themessl-Huber (2007, pp. 432–433) suggest: 'The variations of the action research cycle presented in the literature include circles of action, spirals, varying combinations of circles and spirals and flow diagrams'. At its most basic, action research can be viewed in terms of the processes outlined in Figure 1.1.

This model has its origins in the work of Kurt Lewin (1946) and has been cited in several more recent accounts of action research (e.g. Ritchie *et al.*, 2002; Norton, 2009). From the point of view of teachers and teaching, it involves deciding on a particular focus for research, planning to implement an activity, series of activities, or other interventions, implementing these activities, observing the outcomes, reflecting on what has happened and then

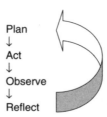

Plan
↓
Act
↓
Observe
↓
Reflect

Figure 1.1 A basic action research model.

planning a further series of activities if necessary. In outlining her own view of the action research cycle, Norton (2009, p. 69) changes the order of the processes in Figure 1.1 and suggests that researchers:

1. observe or notice that something is not as it should be and/or could be improved (observe);
2. plan a course of action which involves changing something in your practice (plan);
3. carry out the change (act);
4. see what effect your change has made (reflect).

Dick (2002) has argued that the action research cycle can be characterised by action leading to critical reflection and then, perhaps, to further action. As he says: 'So action is followed by critical reflection: What worked? What didn't? What have we learned? How might we do it differently next time?' Furthermore: 'Reflection is followed by action. The understanding achieved, the conclusions drawn, the plans developed . . . These are tested in action.'

The action research cycle is further illustrated in Figure 1.2. Here the idea is to demonstrate that, while action research can often involve undertaking a single cycle of planning, acting, observing and reflecting, it can also lead to more lengthy and substantial studies within educational settings.

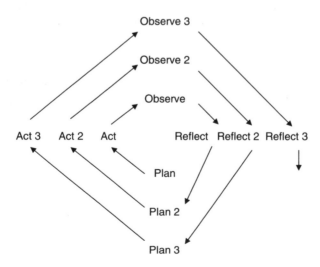

Figure 1.2 An extended action research model.

These may be projects that are undertaken as part of study for a research degree, or funded research projects where the timescale and scope of the research extend beyond what is normally possible to teachers conducting small-scale classroom-based research. If you wish to undertake an action research thesis for an MPhil. or PhD, a number of general and specific texts will be helpful (see, for example, Burgess *et al.*, 2006; Cryer, 2006; Dick, 1993, 2000; Matthiesen and Binder, 2009; Phillips and Pugh, 2005; Trafford and Leshem, 2008; Wellington *et al.*, 2005).

A more elaborate action research model is offered by Michael Bassey, whose framework consists of eight stages which may be summarised as follows (see Bassey, 1998, pp. 94–95 and Robson, 2002, pp. 217–218):

- Stage 1: Defining the enquiry.
- Stage 2: Describing the educational situation.
- Stage 3: Collecting and analysing evaluative data.
- Stage 4: Reviewing the data and looking for contradictions.
- Stage 5: Tackling a contradiction by introducing some aspect of change.
- Stage 6: Monitoring the change.
- Stage 7: Analysing evaluative data concerning the change.
- Stage 8: Reviewing the change and deciding what to do next.

The framework is based on three central questions (Bassey, 1998, p. 94): what is happening in this educational situation of ours now? (Stages 1 to 4); what changes are we going to introduce? (Stage 5); what happens when we make the changes? (Stages 6 to 8).

To accompany these questions and framework, Bassey offers seven invented examples of possible action research projects. For the purposes of illustration, I shall summarise one of these here. The project focuses on an initial question, which defines the inquiry (Stage 1): 'How do I, as head, know what is going on in classrooms?' (p. 96).

In describing the situation (Stage 2), the head teacher indicates that he has recently been appointed to his post. His predecessor tended to manage the school from his room and visited classrooms infrequently. With the intention of providing effective educational leadership, the head teacher begins his action research project (Stage 3) by initiating a discussion among the staff and indicating his proposals for responding to the initial question. Over two weeks, he conducts a ten-minute informal interview with each teacher about the question and makes notes which are agreed with the teacher. He writes a brief paper for staff which summarises the findings and indicates 'a wide range of views from "welcome" to "please keep out"' (p. 96).

The paper is discussed at a staff meeting (Stage 4) and the head teacher attempts to focus on the evident contradiction between his view of his role and the variation of responses made by the staff. At Stage 5, 'Tackle a contradiction by introducing a change', the head indicates his decision to visit classrooms for brief periods, as unobtrusively as possible, to talk with pupils and to look at their work. He says that he will share his thoughts about this process with teachers, on the same day that his visits take place, and he asks them to keep a diary (one brief entry per week) in order to monitor the change (Stage 6).

Another member of staff (possibly the deputy head teacher, although this person is identified only by her initials) offers to read the diaries and to report on staff perceptions of the head teacher's visits (Stage 7). In turn, the head gives his own report about how this process has facilitated his goal of providing appropriate educational leadership. Stage 8 involves reviewing the change and deciding what to do next. This is accomplished at a staff meeting to discuss the reports produced, as a preliminary to agreeing an appropriate course of action.

The final action research model that I shall outline has been produced by Denscombe (2007, p. 126). His framework illustrates the cyclical process in action research and contains five elements: professional practice, critical reflection, research, strategic planning, and action. This model can be represented in several ways and Figure 1.3 outlines one example.

The framework involves beginning with professional practice and reflecting critically on it. Such reflection may lead to the identification of a particular problem or issue that requires research. When this enquiry has been completed, the findings from the research become the starting point for the development of an action plan. Strategic planning leads to instigating change (action), which impacts on professional practice. The cycle then begins again and a further round of critical reflection enables the researcher to evaluate changes made. At this point, conclusions may be drawn and the project may come to an end. However, it is possible that, following the evaluation, some further research may be deemed necessary. If so, the cycle moves on to re-visit this aspect and further 'systematic and rigorous enquiry' (p.126) is undertaken.

1. Professional practice
   ↓
2. Critical reflection
   (identify problem, or
   evaluate changes)
   ↓
3. Research
   (systematic and rigorous
   enquiry)
   ↓
4. Strategic planning
   (translate findings into
   action plan)
   ↓
5. Action
   (instigate change)

Figure 1.3 A representation of Denscombe's action research model.

Some authors have argued that one of the major problems with such research concerns the prescriptive nature of its models, as these may restrict the flexibility with which teachers undertake their studies. For example, Hopkins (2008, p. 55) suggests that 'the tight specification of process steps and cycles may trap teachers within a framework which they may come to depend on and which will, consequently, inhibit independent action'. Hopkins highlights a further problem when he notes that 'the models may appear daunting and confusing to practitioners' (p. 55).

How are we to respond to this critique? To begin with, it should be acknowledged that some action research models are complex both in their design and theoretical justification. Should this lead to misunderstanding or confusion on the part of practitioners, then these models will have failed to achieve their desired purpose: the improvement of educational practice. This said, I would agree with Bob Dick and others that one of the defining characteristics of action research is its cyclical nature. Essentially it focuses, in turn, on action and critical reflection. While this may be represented in the form of a model (or models), it is important to note that practitioners should be offered a range of possible models from which to choose. The emphasis here is on *choice* and not prescription.

I would agree with those who say that choosing a pre-defined framework within which to conduct a research project is, by its very nature, potentially restrictive. However, rather than this being problematic, it is actually an important indicator of a project's likely success. Research projects should be structured soundly and it must be clear from the initial proposal exactly what is being *excluded* from the work to be undertaken as well as what is included.

To opt for action research must involve intention and critical reasoning on the part of the researcher: it is a deliberate choice of a particular type of enquiry. Once this initial choice has been made, practitioners should then decide which action research framework is likely to enable them to achieve their aims and to complete their studies successfully. This involves either selecting from the range of models available or possibly developing one's own model (on the latter option, see McNiff with Whitehead, 2002, p. 55). To argue that researchers should choose or devise a model of action research within which to shape their studies is not, of course, to advocate the *imposition* of particular models, as these may not be 'representative of the realities practitioners will experience. Practitioners need to see these models for what they are: guidelines for how we hope things will eventually fall out' (McNiff with Whitehead, 2002, p. 52). In order to illustrate the choice that is available to researchers, I shall use Denscombe's model to develop three action research projects in Chapter 4, below. Having examined the question 'What is action research?' arguments for undertaking it in educational settings will be explored in the next chapter.

Why Undertake Action Research? **2**

Chapter Outline

The teacher as reflective practitioner	16
Relationships between educational theory and practice	17
The teacher as researcher	20
Teaching as a research-based profession	21
Problems with educational research	21
Teacher research and school improvement	23
Research and teachers' continuing professional development	24
The importance of action research	28

Having offered an account of the nature of action research, my aim in this chapter is to respond to the question 'Why undertake action research?' In order to do this, I shall explore several key themes:

- the teacher as reflective practitioner;
- relationships between educational theory and practice;
- the teacher as researcher;
- teaching as a research-based profession;
- problems with educational research;
- teacher research and school improvement;
- research and teachers' continuing professional development;
- the importance of action research.

The teacher as reflective practitioner

The idea that teachers should be 'reflective practitioners' or should engage in 'reflective practice' has gained popularity due, in large part, to the work of Donald Schön. His books on *The Reflective Practitioner: How Professionals Think in Action* (1991b), *Educating the Reflective Practitioner* (1991a) and *The Reflective Turn: Case Studies in and on Educational Practice* (1992) have a particular relevance for educationalists because of Schön's view that, as practitioners, they should: (1) engage in the study of their own practice; (2) develop their own educational theories deriving from that practice (see McNiff with Whitehead, 2002). Action research provides an appropriate medium to enable these two aims to be achieved.

Here are some authors' accounts of 'reflection', 'reflective practice', and 'reflective teaching' for you to consider.

Reflection

Across many professions (science, nursing, medicine, law, teaching) the need for individuals to develop their understanding about the way they conduct their work, and to be skilled practitioners through their work, has been important in informing the profession about aspects of practice. By so doing, the knowledge base of the profession is developed and refined in ways that help the practitioner to be an effective and informed professional . . . Reflection, then, places an emphasis on learning through questioning and investigation to lead to a development of understanding. (Loughran, 2002, p. 34)

The results of reflection are tangible; changes in the learning process can be seen and felt. Assignments are more thoughtful and result in deeper, fuller understanding, and students bring more meaningful connections to the learning . . . What they have discovered is more likely to become a part of them. Learning becomes an adventure, not an event they must endure . . . A teacher may guide the process with crucial questions or motivating structure, yet ultimately, it is the learner who practises the reflection and who reaps whatever rewards follow. (Hedberg, 2009, p. 31)

Reflective Practice

Reflective practice is learning and developing through examining what we think happened on any occasion, and how we think others perceived the event and us, opening our practice to the scrutiny of others, and studying texts from the wider sphere. (Bolton, 2005, p. 7)

Reflective practice offers one powerful way for educators – individually and collectively – to stay challenged, effective, and alive in their work. The greater the number of people involved, the greater the potential to significantly improve educational practice and, therefore, the greater the potential to enhance student learning. (York-Barr et al., 2006, p. 27)

The purpose of reflective practice is to increase learning at the individual and organisational levels so that educational practice continuously improves and student learning is enhanced. (York-Barr et al., 2006, p. 31)

Reflective Teaching

Reflective teaching implies an active concern with aims and consequences, as well as means and technical efficiency.

Reflective teaching is applied in a cyclical or spiralling process, in which teachers monitor, evaluate and revise their own practice continuously.

Reflective teaching requires competence in methods of evidence-based . . . enquiry, to support the progressive development of higher standards of thinking. (Pollard et al., 2008, p. 14)

Kuit *et al.* (2001, pp. 131–132) refer to action research as a 'method of reflection' and discuss the model of 'plan, act, observe, reflect', which was outlined in Chapter 1:

Planning involves identifying the problem, formulating a hypothesis about the situation, identifying the theory in use and planning the action to be taken. The action is undertaken and observed with data collected. The final stage is reflection, which relates to what the experience means and what can be learnt from it, how can practice match theory, whether the theory needs to be adjusted and whether teaching will change next time.

Relationships between educational theory and practice

I shall discuss relationships between educational theory and practice in Chapter 3, but it is necessary here to make some preliminary comments about this theme. To begin with, we should note that while educational theory and practice are inextricably linked, the relationship between them has been (and continues to be) the subject of keen debate. Since the 1980s, numerous attacks have been made against the theoretical study of education within initial teacher education and training (ITET) courses. For example, in a pamphlet entitled *Who Teaches the Teachers?* Anthony O'Hear (1988, p. 26) suggests that 'what is vital in teaching is practical knowledge combined with emotional maturity and not theoretical knowledge at all'. In a subsequent article, O'Hear indicates the limited value which he attaches to the systematic discussion and evaluation of educational theories. He argues (1989, p. 23) that the theoretical study of education 'should be made available to those teachers who feel a need for it' but suggests that it is more appropriate for practitioners to undertake such study once they have benefited from some experience of the classroom.

Dick (2000) explores an interesting aspect of the theory-practice debate when making a distinction between what he calls 'theory-driven' and 'data-driven' research. In order to illustrate the differences between these two approaches, Dick asks two questions of postgraduate researchers. The first concerns whether they wish to engage in 'research that turns first to a body of extant literature and contributes to knowledge by assuming that literature as a given and extending or refining it, or challenging it?' (a theory-driven perspective). Alternatively, do they want to 'deal with the research situation and the people in it as they are, as far as possible putting aside . . . preconceptions', with a view to 'fully experiencing' the context of the research? This is a data-driven approach.

Proponents of theory-driven research would argue that theory necessarily precedes practice and is applied to it. On this view, before practitioners undertaking action research projects can begin their research, they must engage in a substantial amount of reading (about research methodology; the subject matter of the project; the key theoretical issues that underpin the work; research previously undertaken in this field etc.). Only then, having considered such key issues carefully, can researchers begin their own studies.

However, advocates of a data-driven approach suggest that, in order to undertake research, a greater degree of flexibility is required than is permitted by the theory-driven perspective. For example, it is argued that any prescriptive requirement for researchers to conduct an extensive preliminary review of the literature may lead to them selecting a focus for their work which is restricted by the findings of that review. In turn, this may stifle the potential of researchers to be creative when completing projects, because they may feel the need to remain within the parameters of the research as it was initially conceived, rather than being able to respond more imaginatively and spontaneously as the project progresses. Secondly, it is suggested that important areas for investigation actually arise from research data collected and that these potential avenues for research might not have been considered by an initial literature review.

Dick (2000) notes that it is the data-driven approach to action research which is of most interest to him because of its perceived flexibility and responsiveness to the research context. He also makes a distinction between what he calls 'the researcher as technician' and 'the researcher as performing artist'. The former he likens to an apprentice who learns from his/her tutor and from the relevant literature how to adopt a particular approach to research.

The second type of researcher is described as someone who undertakes research 'with whatever resources and understanding [he/she] can bring to bear' and who learns from the experience. Dick indicates that these two perspectives involve a shift in the teaching-learning interface and, conse-quently, in the tutor-student relationship. He suggests that the conception of the 'researcher as performing artist' involves learning mainly through 'questioning enquiry', in a context where the tutor acts as a mentor rather than as a teacher.

What are we to make of these two sets of distinctions (theory-driven versus data-driven research and the researcher as technician versus the researcher as performing artist)? I would argue that there is no need to choose between the alternatives offered in either case, as each has its own merits and strengths. Essentially, I would want to ask the following questions: Why can research not be both theory- and data-driven? Why is it not possible to view the researcher as, in some sense, both an apprentice and (at least potentially) a performing artist?

Action research undertaken for an academic award is essentially and inevitably a form of apprenticeship and success depends on one's ability to do several things with a certain degree of skill. However, as we shall see in the following chapters of this book, the competencies and skills required to enable practitioners to complete projects to a high standard can be taught and learned. Furthermore, while technical proficiency is certainly an essential prerequisite for success, this does not preclude critical, reflective enquiry.

Indeed, the ability and willingness to ask pertinent questions, to test assumptions, to ask for reasons and evidence to support arguments, and to engage in systematic thinking about educational theories and practices, are essential attributes of the researcher (and this irrespective of whether the activities engaged in are conceived of as being theory- or data-driven).

Reflective Thinking Exercise 2.1 invites you to offer your own view of the key themes addressed so far in this chapter.

Reflective Thinking Exercise 2.1

1. What do you consider is meant by the term 'reflective practitioner'?
2. Outline three examples of reflective practice in which you have engaged.
3. What is the relationship between educational theory and practice?

The teacher as researcher

A focus on relationships between educational theory and practice leads us on to consider the notion of 'the teacher as researcher'. While the idea that teachers should be regarded as researchers, or as practitioner-researchers (see Robson, 2002, Appendix B), is now becoming increasingly popular, several authors point out that this is not a recent idea. Hopkins (2008) offers a concise account of the origins of the teacher research movement, beginning with the work of Lawrence Stenhouse, who directed the Schools Council's Humanities Curriculum Project and authored a number of key publications, including *An Introduction to Curriculum Research and Development* (1975) and 'What counts as research?' (1981).

Substantial contributions to the development of teacher research were also made by John Elliott and Clem Adelman through the Ford Teaching Project, which involved 40 primary and secondary school teachers completing action research projects that focused on classroom-based practice. As Hopkins (2008, p. 1) points out: 'These teachers developed hypotheses about their teaching which could be shared with other teachers and used to enhance their own teaching'.

Teaching as a research-based profession

More recent initiatives in advancing the cause of teacher research include the proposal that teaching should move increasingly towards being a research-based profession (Hargreaves, 1996, 1999; Radford, 2006). In addition, both Campbell (2007) and Coleman (2007) offer examples of the broad support which exists, across a number of organisations and other agencies, for practitioner-based enquiry. Such enquiry involves practitioners undertaking research activity as an important aspect of their role, with a view to gathering data about a range of issues including strategies for effective learning and teaching.

Rose (2002, p. 45) summarises some of the key arguments offered by Stenhouse (1981) in the article referred to above. It is interesting to note, three decades later, the extent to which these themes are now very much in vogue. Stenhouse suggests that teachers should be at the forefront of educational research and that classrooms provide an ideal context within which to test educational theories. He argues that unless teachers are fully involved in research being undertaken, they will not wish to be consumers of the findings that emerge from it. Furthermore, teachers have lacked opportunities (other than those offered within higher degree courses) to take on a more substantial role in the research process. Finally, on the traditional view of educational research, practitioners have been asked to justify themselves and their practices to researchers. However, according to Stenhouse, it is researchers who should be offering justifications to practitioners.

Problems with educational research

More recently, the nature, purposes and future of educational research have been the focus of critical scrutiny (see Gorard, 2004; 2005; Hillage *et al.*, 1998; Tooley with Darby, 1998). As Foskett *et al.* (2005, p. 245) suggest:

> Reflecting on the current state of research in any academic discipline is an important part of its evolution and development. A consideration of the relevance and utility of research and the added value that accrues to society from its products provides key benchmarks for all in the research community. For those of us who work in 'second order fields' . . . such as educational research, where

> we are researching activity in 'first order fields' (e.g. the professional world of education) these considerations become of especial significance. Without a clear payoff for our research in terms of enhancing policy and practice, however measured . . . researchers will surely be doomed to an existence that is marginal in both academic and professional arenas.

Criticisms made of educational research include the following (see, for example, Hargreaves, 1996; Rose, 2002). First, there is a widening gulf between researchers and classroom practitioners, and research often fails to focus on 'the real life experiences of most teachers' (Rose, 2002, p. 44). Second, for the most part, research is an activity or series of activities which is done *to* practitioners, rather than *by* them. Third, the findings of research are often published in obscure journals, that are inaccessible to teachers both in terms of the style in which they are written and their location (usually the library of a higher education institution (HEI)). This is inconsistent with a central aim of educational journals: to improve practice in schools and classrooms.

A fourth criticism of educational research focuses on the tendency for it to be compared unfavourably with other, supposedly more rigorous, forms of research. For example, Riehl (2006, p. 24) notes that the federal government in the USA has attempted 'to move education research in more "scientific" directions'. Furthermore, she suggests that 'In their efforts to improve the quality and persuasiveness of education research, many researchers and research-focused policy makers have advocated increased use of experimental methods, especially randomised experiments' (p.24). Burkhardt and Schoenfeld (2003, p. 3) quote the following statement from the U.S. Department of Education's Strategic Plan for 2002–2007:

> Unlike medicine, agriculture and industrial production, the field of education operates largely on the basis of ideology and professional consensus. As such, it is subject to fads and is incapable of the cumulative progress that follows from the application of the scientific method and from the systematic collection and use of objective information in policy making. We will change education to make it an evidence-based field.

Slavin (2002, p. 15), in focusing on the transformation of educational practice and research, begins by offering the following scathing comment: 'At the dawn of the 21st century, educational research is finally entering the 20th century'. He goes on to discuss 'the promise and pitfalls of randomised and rigorously matched experiments as a basis for policy and practice in education' and concludes by arguing that 'a focus on rigorous experiments evaluating replicable programmes and practices is essential to build confidence in educational research among policymakers and educators' (p. 15).

Teacher research and school improvement

How are we to respond to these criticisms? I shall discuss the issue of rigour in action research in Chapter 4. It seems to me that the best way to answer the first three criticisms involves demonstrating the important effects that teacher research in general, and action research in particular, may have both on school improvement and on practitioners' professional development. As regards the first issue, Rob Halsall (1998) outlines the case for teacher research as a strategy for school improvement. Interestingly, the sub-title of his book is *Opening Doors from the Inside* and the volume contains a number of case studies (some written by teachers themselves) that outline the impact of research at whole school, department and classroom levels (see also Carter and Halsall, 1998).

Foskett *et al.* (2005, p. 247) refer to a survey of schools which found that '96 per cent of respondents had seriously considered research since qualifying [to teach]. Much of the research was received through the filters of training courses and via government departments, but nearly two-thirds of respondents had consulted journals. Of this group, 69 per cent appeared to have been influenced in their practice'.

The aim of Reflective Thinking Exercise 2.2 is to encourage you to draw on your professional experience to evaluate the importance of educational research.

Reflective Thinking Exercise 2.2

1. What do you consider to be the value of educational research?
2. Can you identify a piece of educational research that has had an impact on your own professional practice?
3. Should teachers undertake research to evaluate and improve their own practice?

Research and teachers' continuing professional development

The relationship between research and teachers' professional development is a close one (Coleman, 2007). Indeed, a welcome and much-needed debate has been taking place about the nature of continuing professional development (CPD) for teachers and how this might be improved. For example, the General Teaching Council for Wales (GTCW) (2002a), in a document entitled *Continuing Professional Development: an Entitlement for All*, offered advice to the National Assembly for Wales concerning a range of issues. The GTCW argued that 'all teachers should be entitled to high quality and well-planned CPD provision throughout their career' (para. 19). However, such an entitlement carries with it certain responsibilities: 'to develop oneself professionally and to ensure that professional knowledge and skills are constantly updated' (para. 19). It is noted (para. 14) that: 'CPD activities take many forms. These range from attending courses to school-based learning and undertaking action research'. As Coleman (2007, p. 482) has noted: 'The increased commitment to . . . CPD for teachers . . . has also led to greater emphasis being placed on self-assessment and reflection as mechanisms for enhancing personal performance'.

Hargreaves (1996) suggested that the gulf between educational researchers and classroom practitioners constitutes a serious problem, as well as being '. . . an obstacle which prevents educational research making a significant contribution to theory or knowledge' (Rose, 2002, p.45). Against this backdrop, the introduction of the Best Practice Research Scholarship programme in England (Furlong and Salisbury, 2005; Prestage *et al.*, 2002) and the Teacher Research Scholarship scheme in Wales (Costello, 2007a) was widely welcomed. Funded and managed by the GTCW, the latter initiative commenced in 2001–2. It has enabled teachers to undertake small-scale action research projects focusing on topics and themes, issues and problems, questions and hypotheses, which *they* regarded as important and so wished to investigate.

Examples of completed research project titles are:

- Improving well-being and the involvement of pre-school children with behaviour problems.
- Gender and reading for pleasure.

- Does the use of interactive ICT improve historical skills in pupils?
- An exploration of how creative writing can be improved in a Year 5 class.
- How can circle time be used in the primary school to improve children's self-esteem?
- Investigating the effectiveness of a Student Assistance Programme in a junior school.

I have acted as a mentor to two groups of teachers who received GTCW scholarships. The first group, based within Wrexham Local Education Authority, undertook action research projects in a broad range of areas. The second, also sponsored by the National Union of Teachers, completed projects on the teaching and learning of thinking skills in infant and secondary schools. This involved attendance at two residential seminars, where teachers were introduced to aspects of research methodology, issues relating to thinking skills, the development of research projects, data collection and analysis, and writing research reports.

The GTCW TRS scheme was evaluated in two ways. Firstly, comprehensive reports were produced by Egan and James (2002, 2003, and 2004). The first of these involved the development of an evaluation pro forma for teacher researchers; a questionnaire concerning the effectiveness of the scheme, which was sent to their head teachers; a questionnaire for tutors/mentors; and a series of interviews with teacher researchers, head teachers and line-managers. The report (p. 15) indicated the following benefits to teachers from undertaking action research projects: the development of individual needs and skills; motivational and career factors; engagement with good practice; time to develop reflective practice; work-based learning; working collaboratively with other professionals; and learning and teaching gains.

In addition, I undertook my own evaluation of the impact of TRS on enhancing teachers' professional development. Following the evaluation pro forma produced by Egan and James, I asked the following questions to two cohorts of teachers (15 respondents in all):

- How effective do you consider the chosen activity to be in enhancing your professional knowledge, skills and expertise? Please circle your response (1 = very effective; 4 = very ineffective)

  1   2   3   4

  Please comment briefly:

  _____

  _____

  _____

- How could you further develop the work you have undertaken? Please specify.

  _____

  _____

  _____

In answer to the first question, 12 respondents indicated a '1' and 3 indicated a '2'. Written comments included the following:

- It has made me look at what I do 'day in, day out'. I haven't really been doing anything new, but I have become aware of what I'm doing and have looked at the results of my strategies in the teaching and learning process. I have probably become even more aware of the needs of the pupils I teach and the need to continue to look for new ideas. I have most certainly become more confident in myself and it has given me the 'feel good factor'.
- Time to read and to research. Networking and sharing practice. Focus on mentoring: I feel confident to undertake more research. Focus on learning and teaching in general: I have adapted ideas from target groups to other classes.
- The research project has been excellent in enhancing my professional development, as prior to this I was not even aware of what thinking skills were, let alone being able to implement them in my classroom. It is also an opportunity to undertake research which is directly related to improving teaching and thus learning.
- Very effective. The first course produced new ideas. The research process helped me to develop thinking skills strategies and spread them through the Faculty. It improved my skills and those of other teachers within the Faculty.
- I have enjoyed working on my research project and have developed various skills which will enhance my teaching – such as improved questioning techniques.
- Very effective because it's given me the drive to read about 'thinking skills' and provided me with the opportunity to work with my colleagues.
- The project has given me insight into the way that my pupils think about the work they do. I hope that by providing them with a 'thinking skills' exercise, they will become more proficient at thinking while working.
- It has allowed me to focus on thinking skills and begin to understand how I might develop my teaching to use techniques and information to my (and my students') advantage.

Responses to the second question included the following:

- I would like to have the opportunity to 'spread' my experiences across the school and to work with other teachers within the [Local Authority] and further afield. I would like to be supported in doing some further written work (e.g. a teacher's handbook for classroom management).
- Adapt my research and findings to other areas of the scheme of work.
- I wish to develop further thinking skills strategies within the classroom and perhaps extend to a whole school approach across key stages. It would also be useful to do

another research project which could build on the one already undertaken – perhaps to implement thinking skills across the curriculum.

- I would like to form a working group within the school to develop thinking skills activities across the curriculum, in order to spread good practice.
- I now want to continue my research and spread good practice across the whole school. Thinking skills should be a key area in whole-school curriculum development. I personally would like to initiate this and research my findings.
- Develop professional debate among staff to enhance the learning community.

The GTCW (2002a, para. 26) suggests that 'Conditions need to be created . . . to allow [teachers] to be reflective – to learn, develop, and improve as an integral part of their work'. Furthermore, 'There is a need to provide teachers with time to plan, undertake, reflect [on] and disseminate their experiences. This best takes place in environments that foster learning'.

The importance of action research

In order to answer the question, 'Why undertake action research?' I have examined a number of related issues. Considering these together enables us to offer several statements indicating the importance of action research. To begin with, reflective practitioners are concerned to study their own practice and action research provides an excellent medium for this to take place. Second, action research enables practitioners to explore relationships between educational theory and practice. Third, the critical scrutiny of educational research has led to an increasing emphasis on the importance of practitioners undertaking their own research studies. Fourth, a move towards developing teaching as a research-based profession should lead practitioners to:

1. take an increasingly prominent role in the processes of gathering and analysing research data, and reporting research findings;
2. complete action research projects regularly (and not only as part of higher degree courses).

Finally, action research can have a beneficial impact both on school improvement and on the professional development of teachers. Before we move on to the development of action research projects, which will be discussed in

Chapter 3, please consider the questions outlined in Reflective Thinking Exercise 2.3.

Reflective Thinking Exercise 2.3

1. What is the relationship between reflective thinking and practice?
2. What is the relationship between reflective practice and action research?
3. Why undertake action research?

How Do I Develop an Action Research Project?

Chapter Outline

Choosing a research topic   31
Developing a research proposal   32
Undertaking a literature search and review   33
Working with your tutor   35
Undertaking action research projects: some preliminary considerations   42

In order to illustrate the development of an action research project, including data collection and analysis, I shall outline three extended examples in Chapters 4 and 5 below. However, my purpose here is to focus on some general issues concerning:

- choosing a research topic;
- developing a research proposal;
- undertaking a literature search and review;
- working with your tutor;
- research methodology courses and seminars;
- undertaking action research projects: some preliminary considerations.

Choosing a research topic

In focusing on the central question: 'How do I develop an action research project?' you may already have a research topic in mind. If this is not the case, you might like to consider possibilities for research outlined by, for example, Bassey (1998, pp. 96– 107); Macintyre (2000, pp. 32– 41); Mertler (2009, p. 22); and Wragg (1999, pp.110– 111). As Wragg (p. 110) indicates, there is a wide range of potential research topics. These include:

- What do teachers and pupils do in the classroom; how do they spend their time?
- What kind of interaction takes place, who talks to whom and about what?
- How do teachers manage their classes; what are the classroom rules; how are elements such as time, space, pupil behaviour, or their own teaching strategies managed?
- What do pupils learn; what tasks do they engage in, and with what degree of involvement and success?
- What happens to particularly able pupils or those with learning difficulties?
- How are classroom decisions made, by the teacher, by pupils, by both in negotiation?
- What happens when pupils disrupt lessons or behave in an anti-social manner?
- How can I improve my own teaching?

Please consider the issues and questions set out in Reflective Thinking Exercise 3.1.

Reflective Thinking Exercise 3.1

1. Write down two possible research project topics.
2. Why are you interested in these topics?
3. In undertaking a research project in these areas, what do you want to find out?
4. Which topic do you prefer?
5. Why?

Developing a research proposal

Once you have determined an appropriate subject or context for research, it is necessary to draw up a research proposal. Usually, this will be reviewed by your tutor (or, in certain circumstances, by a review committee). However, if you are undertaking a funded research project, you will be required to submit a proposal to the funding body.

In preparing an action research proposal for your tutor, you may be asked to write a brief outline (no more than two or three A4 pages) containing the following information:

- Your name.
- A tentative title for the project (this may be amended in consultation with your tutor).
- The aims of your project.
- Possible research questions for your project.
- The educational setting or context within which your project will be undertaken.
- The period of time within which your project will be undertaken.
- The research methodology you propose to use.
- Anticipated outcomes of your research.
- An outline bibliography.

This information will provide a context for your first meeting with your tutor. Putting it together in the way I have suggested will involve you in some preliminary reflection and research. This is an essential aspect of the process and a thorough approach at this stage will enable you to develop a solid foundation for the project as a whole.

Undertaking a literature search and review

To begin with, you need to undertake a literature search (Hart, 2001; Rumsey, 2008). The purpose of this is to establish whether the research topic you are proposing is a viable one. If you are unable to gain access to a sufficient amount of reading, both to deepen your understanding of the chosen field of study and to underpin the research you will undertake, your tutor or the review committee is likely to suggest that you choose a more appropriate topic.

In order to complete an effective literature search, you need to become familiar with your HEI's library. This involves

- reading the library's guidelines on searching for appropriate resources;
- exploring the library's general catalogue of resources;
- finding information about your subject discipline (including information on books; electronic books (e-books); journals; online databases; the Internet (including

Internet Gateways); reference collections; audiovisual material (videos and DVDs) and newspapers.

As regards Internet Gateways, you may find the following useful:

- *Current Education and Children's Services Research (CERUK)*: a database of current educational research projects. Available at: http://www.ceruk.ac.uk.
- *Education-line*: a database of conference papers, working papers and electronic literature supporting educational research, policy and practice. Available at: http://www.leeds.ac.uk/bei/index.html.
- *Intute: Education and Research Methods*: a database of Internet websites to assist you with your research. Available at: http://www.intute.ac.uk/education/.
- *Teacher Training Resource Bank*: this website includes articles focusing on action research projects undertaken in schools. Available at: http://www.ttrb.ac.uk.

Having completed the literature search, you can begin the process of literature review (Cridland, 2008; Hart, 1998; Mertler, 2009). This is necessary because your action research project needs to demonstrate relationships between educational theory and practice, which involves examining critically what authors have to say about educational issues, and applying the reasons, evidence, arguments or proof they offer to the practical context of the classroom, school or other educational setting.

In reviewing the relevant literature (books, chapters in edited books, journal articles, Internet sources etc.), an important aim is to enable you to offer answers to key questions such as: 'When authors tell me what is happening (or should) happen in, for example, a classroom, does this coincide with my own experience? If yes, why? If no, why not? As a result of this review, do I need to investigate the possibility of introducing appropriate change into my classroom? If yes, how might I do this?' Reflective Thinking Exercise 3.2 will help you to reflect on the aims and purposes of a literature review.

Reflective Thinking Exercise 3.2

1. Consider the following statements about the review of literature.
2. What do these accounts have in common?
3. What are the distinctive features of each account?

The aim of a literature review is to show your reader (your tutor) that you have read, and have a good grasp of, the main published work concerning a particular topic or question in your field. This work may be in any format, including online sources. (Birmingham City University, 2007)

The purpose of the literature review:

1. To select research relevant to my study.
2. To outline existing knowledge in my field.
3. To evaluate existing research relevant to my field.
4. To identify research methods relevant to my study.
5. To identify gaps in the research.
6. To identify more appropriate research methods.
7. To position my study in the context of previous research.
8. To express views about the topic.
9. To indicate how my topic is to be investigated.
10. To justify my study.

(Cridland, 2008)

By reviewing related literature, you can identify a topic, narrow its focus, and gather information for developing a research design, as well as the overall project . . . A review of literature can reveal a study that could be systematically replicated in your classroom or provide you with potential solutions to the research problem you have identified. The literature review can also help establish a connection between your action research project and what others have said, done, and discovered before you . . . A literature review allows you to use the insights and discoveries of others whose research came before yours in order to make your research more efficient and effective. (Mertler, 2009, p. 51)

Working with your tutor

At your first meeting with your tutor, you will have an opportunity to: discuss your proposal; indicate why you think it is an important area for research; outline its key aims; and convince the tutor that you have access both to an appropriate educational setting (e.g. a classroom) and to sufficient theoretical resources (books, journal articles etc.) to complete the project successfully. During the meeting, your tutor may suggest some amendments to your proposal or he/she may ask you to give further thought to aspects of it, with a view to finalising the outline at the next meeting. As a result of these initial meetings, you will produce an agreed strategy for undertaking the project.

At this stage, you may have a number of queries about your research and it is important to make your tutor aware of these. Never be afraid to ask questions: these are essential to ensuring a successful outcome for your work. There are several reasons why you may be reluctant to ask your tutor to clarify key issues. First, you may not wish your tutor (or anyone else) to know that you require additional guidance or support. Second, you may have several questions and do not wish to trouble your tutor with them. Third, you may not wish to ask questions in front of your fellow practitioners. Fourth, you may generally be unsure both about what is required of you and how to indicate this uncertainty to your tutor.

Whatever the reason for such reluctance, you should avail yourself of all opportunities that are provided to meet your tutor and to articulate any concerns you may have. By doing this, you are much more likely to complete your project successfully. In addition, you may save both yourself and your tutor a great deal of time in the long-term because regular discussions should lead to fewer errors or misconceptions either in developing or carrying out your research.

If you do not wish to ask questions in front of others, arrange to meet your tutor to discuss these or see him/her during a seminar break or at the end of a teaching session. Never assume that your questions are so naïve or lacking in complexity that you would be reluctant to ask them. Please remember that your tutor is as concerned as you are to ensure your success. Eliminating uncertainties at the beginning of a project, or as they arise once it is underway, will do much to accomplish this goal.

Please complete Reflective Thinking Exercise 3.3, which focuses on developing your draft research proposal.

Reflective Thinking Exercise 3.3

1. Using the headings above (or those suggested by your tutor/HEI), write a draft research proposal.
2. In completing the outline bibliography, ensure that you include some current journal articles.
3. Discuss the proposal with your tutor.

Research methodology courses and seminars

In order to enable you to complete your research project, it is usual for HEIs to provide modules or a series of seminars on research methodology. Typically, these focus on topics such as: undertaking a research project; working with your tutor; choosing an appropriate research methodology; reading for, planning and writing your research project; citation and referencing; and presenting your research project.

I have already outlined some aspects of working with your tutor. In addition, it is important to attend research methods seminars (if these are provided) and again to ask questions when you are unsure about anything that is being discussed or outlined. When teaching research methodology courses, I begin by offering students a sheet with three headings:

1. Things I know about undertaking the research project.
2. Things I am not sure about in undertaking the research project.
3. Things I would like to know about undertaking the research project.

They are invited to write up to five comments under each of these. Then I collate responses and ensure that all aspects mentioned under the latter two headings are discussed. During the final seminar, there is an opportunity for course members to ask any remaining questions and for me to revise key themes as necessary. Issues and questions commonly raised in the first seminars are:

- I'm not sure what a research project is.
- What are the differences between a project and an assignment?
- What is action research?
- Am I the only one who feels apprehensive about tackling a research project?
- What is the best way to start?
- What am I going to focus on?
- From whom should I seek help/advice?
- How much time will I have with my project tutor?
- Will I be given assistance to get started and will I have the opportunity to discuss the project on a one-to-one basis?
- Will I be supervised so that, if I am in danger of going wrong, I will be told and helped well in advance of the hand-in date?

- Can I see completed research projects?
- What kind of questions should I be asking?
- Is classroom-based research optional, necessary, or essential?
- Do I have to undertake interviews/questionnaires?
- Does every chapter have to have a title?
- How should I go about research and incorporate it into my project report?
- I am worried about: (1) plagiarism; (2) use of other people's ideas and putting them in my own words.
- Use of quotations/citations in the text.
- Can we use footnotes or will we use the Harvard system of referencing?
- Presentation of the bibliography.
- Do I need appendices? Where do I put them in my research report?
- Is my project title appropriate? Should the title be a question or a statement?
- How should I use my school experience placements/teaching experience in developing my project?
- Relationship between educational theory and practice.
- How often should I quote?
- What should the conclusion contain?
- Where do I find the information/resources?
- Continuity between chapters.
- Presentation of the report.
- How do I get a good mark or grade?

Your own HEI will provide you with a set of guidelines concerning the completion of the research project. If, having reviewed these guidelines, you have questions about them, or about any of the issues and questions outlined above, please ask your tutor for clarification.

While you are undertaking your project, your tutor will wish to meet you, either individually or with a small group of other researchers, in order to review your progress. As I have indicated above, attendance at such meetings, whether or not they are compulsory, is also important to your success and allows your tutor to determine whether you need additional guidance in completing the research. As your work progresses, you may be asked to:

1. submit draft chapters for your tutor to read and comment on;
2. produce a complete draft of your report before submitting the final version.

Again, although this may be optional, it is important to take advantage of the opportunities that are being offered.

If you are undertaking a funded research project, your proposal to the funding body is likely to have a format which is similar to that outlined by the GTCW (2002b). Applicants for TRS are asked to complete a proposal of between 500 and 700 words which outlines the following: the title of the research project; the aims of the research project; a statement concerning how the research project will help to raise educational standards; the expected outcomes of the research project, both for the researcher and his/her school; the research methodology to be used; the timescale and schedule for the research project, including anticipated milestones; how the research undertaken will be evaluated; the total funding requested and a breakdown of costs to be incurred.

Funding bodies usually require researchers to have academic support in undertaking their projects. This is provided by a mentor from a local education authority, HEI, subject association, or research body, etc. The mentor may assist researchers to develop their initial proposal, as well as offer guidance through regular meetings, workshops, residential seminars, or via e-mail correspondence. Mentors may also agree to read and comment on work in progress, including draft copies of research reports.

Funded projects differ in one important respect from those undertaken as part of a course of study for an academic qualification: they are primarily practical pieces of research. Given this, practitioners are not expected to undertake a formal review of the relevant literature before completing their studies. Nevertheless, some engagement with the literature may be very beneficial, as it is likely to suggest possible topics or themes for research, as well as deepening the researchers' knowledge and understanding of key aspects of the work to be undertaken.

In the next chapter, I shall discuss a number of possible criticisms that may be made of action research. In attempting to counter these, I shall argue that researchers should endeavour to make their work as rigorous as possible. Examining the relevant literature, even if only briefly, and applying some of the insights derived from it to the context of current or proposed projects, should lead to more rigorous research being completed. This is the best way to respond to those sceptics who are doubtful about the value of small-scale practitioner research.

Before outlining the three action research projects I mentioned at the beginning of this chapter, I want to return to the list of issues and questions commonly raised by undergraduate and postgraduate students. If you are unsure about what a research project is, guidance will be provided either in research methodology seminars, or by your tutor. Basically, a research project is a long essay in which you undertake:

1. a critical review of the relevant literature concerning your proposed topic;
2. practical research within a classroom, school, or other educational setting.

Projects may vary in length both between academic courses and HEIs.

One difference between a research project and an assignment is that the former tends to be a longer piece of work. When faced with writing a research study of several thousand words, it is quite natural to feel some apprehension. However, this can be significantly reduced through attendance at appropriate seminars, by working closely with your tutor in the ways I have suggested above, and by looking at examples of successfully completed projects.

You should be given opportunities to examine research reports produced by students in previous years. This may be a formal part of a research methodology course, or you may be asked to look at projects in your own time (they may be housed in your HEI's library). This is a valuable exercise, as it gives you the opportunity to consider questions such as:

- What are appropriate topics for research projects?
- What do successful research project reports look like (format, contents, presentation etc.)?
- What are the titles of research projects?
- How are chapters or sections of project reports structured?
- How do chapters or sections of project reports relate to each other?
- Do researchers provide reviews of the relevant literature?
- Do researchers justify their choice of research methodology?
- How do researchers gather data?
- How do researchers analyse data?
- How are research project reports presented?

Please consider Reflective Thinking Exercise 3.4.

Reflective Thinking Exercise 3.4

1. Read three research project reports.
2. In each case, write a critical evaluation of the report, detailing its strengths and areas for improvement.
3. What have you learned from this exercise?

Most research projects are intended to enable you to use your teaching experience or school experience placements to good effect. Ideally, you should focus on an aspect or aspects of teaching that interest you. For example, if you are a trainee teacher, you will need to discuss the precise focus of your research with your school mentor. If you are required to make some preliminary visits to the school before your placement begins, make sure that the mentor is aware that you have to complete a project and seek his/her guidance about how best to proceed. Usually, the mentor will have experience of working with students undertaking research studies and so will be an important source of support.

If you are undertaking an action research project as part of another academic qualification (such as a Master's degree in Education), try to ensure that the topic you select enables you to make the most of the educational context in which you find yourself. For example, for the teacher, classrooms and schools are rich sources of potential research studies. Many research proposals are based on aspects of teaching and learning and emerge from practitioners' own reflection on their practice or on the academic progress of their pupils.

If you are about to begin a Master's dissertation, your choice of topic will usually emerge from the taught modules that have made up the first part of your degree. Having explored a number of topics and issues, and completed assignments in these areas, you may choose to focus on one theme in considerable depth. Most probably, you will not have experience of writing such a lengthy project report. The best way to approach this task is to consider that you are writing five or six shorter, though connected, essays. Think carefully about the title and the content to be covered in each chapter.

Having produced a proposal and agreed its basic content and structure with your tutor, you should write a draft chapter (often a review of the literature). The feedback you receive from your tutor will be useful because it should: confirm whether or not the chapter is of an appropriate standard for success; indicate those aspects of the chapter which are satisfactory or better as they stand; outline those aspects where improvements could be made; and detail those aspects which require further work. At this stage, it is advisable to consider carefully the advice that you are given. If you are unsure about any aspect of it, please consult your tutor. Once you have made appropriate amendments, a second draft should be submitted, together with the first. Sending both versions to your tutor will enable him/her to see quickly how you have responded to the suggestions made.

Undertaking action research projects: some preliminary considerations

Prior to proceeding with your action research project, I suggest that you should:

- Undertake reading on research methodology (the bibliography of this book provides a good starting point).
- Consult completed research project reports.
- Undertake a literature search, enabling confirmation (both to yourself and to your tutor) that you have access to a sufficient amount of educational theory to underpin your research. Note that a literature search, though not required for small-scale funded research, may be very useful.
- Write an outline of your proposed project, including a rationale for it and an account of your suggested research methodology.
- Detail the contents of your research project report, either chapter by chapter or section by section (this may be amended during your research).

Having begun your research project, you should:

- Meet your tutor/mentor regularly to discuss your project.
- Produce individual draft chapters/sections of the project report for your tutor to read. This is preferable to submitting several chapters/sections at the same time because, if

there are problems with one chapter, it is likely that these will be replicated in other chapters too).

- Ensure continuity between chapters or sections of the project report. I shall discuss this further in Chapter 6.

In the next chapter, issues concerning the collection of action research data will be explored.

How Do I Collect Action Research Data?

4

Chapter Outline

Collecting action research data: some preliminary considerations   45

Rigour in action research   52

Examples of action research projects   57

Here and in the following chapter, I shall outline three invented examples of action research projects. In devising these examples, my aim is to offer illustrations that demonstrate the following:

- relationships between educational theory and practice;
- relationships between quantitative and qualitative research;
- a variety of approaches to collecting action research data;
- rigour in action research.

Collecting action research data: some preliminary considerations

Before undertaking an action research project and collecting data, you should be aware of the main criticisms that have been made of action research as a mode of enquiry (for example, the prescriptive nature of its models, as discussed in Chapter 1). If you are completing a project as part of a course of study for an academic qualification, you will need to demonstrate your understanding of these criticisms. You will also need to offer suggestions as to how action researchers in general (and you in particular, in the context of your own research) have sought to overcome them. Depending on the nature of your study, it may also be important to explore some problems associated with the practice of educational research in its broadest sense, and these I have discussed in Chapter 2. Concerns about and criticisms of action research have tended to focus on:

- ethical concerns associated with undertaking action research projects;
- rigour in action research.

Let us examine these issues in turn.

Ethical issues

Denscombe (2007, p. 128) outlines a number of ethical issues which practitioners should consider when undertaking action research projects. He argues that a particular problem facing action researchers concerns the fact that while their projects tend to focus on their own activities, 'it is almost inevitable that the activity of colleagues will also come under the microscope at some stage or other'. This is because practitioners do not work in isolation: 'Their practice and the changes they seek to make can hardly be put in place without some knock-on effect for others who operate close-by in organisational terms' (p. 128) (see also Denscombe, 2009, Chapter 4).

What are the implications of this for researchers? First, they should distinguish between undertaking action research that is personal to them and that focuses on their own practice, and research that relates to, and impacts on, the work of others. Where the latter is inevitable, 'the usual standards of research ethics must be observed: permissions obtained, confidentiality maintained, identities protected' (Denscombe, 2007, p. 129). Denscombe suggests that practitioners should be open about their research and that they should ensure that those involved in it give informed consent to what is being proposed. In particular, permission should be sought before researchers engage in any form of observation or examine documentation that may have been produced for purposes other than the research project.

Chapters 6 and 8 of this book focus on the questions: 'How do I produce an action research report?' and 'How do I publish my action research report?' Here, too, as Denscombe acknowledges, ethical considerations are important, since researchers should ensure that any descriptions of others' works or the viewpoints they offer (for example, during interviews) must be agreed with the parties concerned before reports are submitted for examination or publication.

Before undertaking an undergraduate or postgraduate research project, it is likely that you will be asked by your HEI to complete an ethical approval form. Typically, this is divided into several sections, the first of which asks you to provide basic information such as your name, e-mail address and research project title. This may be followed by a preliminary checklist, as well as a section in which you outline the details of your project (see Figures 4.1 and 4.2). Please note that HEIs often provide a generic ethical approval form, that is, one which is used across a broad range of subject disciplines. The checklist is an amended version of the document used by my own university and, in my experience, most undergraduate and postgraduate research projects involve the researcher in answering 'yes' to questions 1 to 3 and 'no' to the remaining questions.

If you are undertaking research within a setting such as a school, you may be asked to provide an information sheet for the head teacher and a consent form for him/her to sign (see Figures 4.3 and 4.4). As regards the last item on the information sheet, 'How research data will be stored and used', I ask my students to write the following statement: 'Two copies of the research project will be given to my tutor; one will be returned to me and one kept by my tutor. I shall ensure that confidentiality, privacy and anonymity of data are maintained at all times'. When completed, all of this documentation, which will usually be checked by your tutor, should be placed in the appendices of your research report. I shall discuss this further in Chapter 6.

Reflective Thinking Exercise 4.1 focuses on the issue of gaining ethical approval for your research project.

Reflective Thinking Exercise 4.1

Find out whether you need to complete an ethical approval form.

1. If so, read this carefully, together with any associated documentation.
2. Ensure you understand what is required of you and discuss any queries you may have with your tutor.

Research Project Proposal		
Preliminary Checklist (please tick boxes ✔)		
	YES	NO
Does the study involve participants who are particularly vulnerable (e.g. young children)?		
Does the study involve participants who would find it difficult to give informed consent (e.g. young children, people with learning difficulties)?		
Will the study require the co-operation of a gatekeeper for initial access to the groups or individuals to be recruited?		
Will it be necessary for participants to take part in the study without their knowledge or consent at the time?		
Will the study involve discussion of topics which the participants may find sensitive?		
Are drugs, placebos or other substances to be administered to the study participants?		
Will the study involve invasive, intrusive or potentially harmful procedures of any kind?		
Will blood or tissue samples be obtained from participants?		
Is pain or more than mild discomfort likely to result from the study?		
Could the study induce psychological distress or anxiety or cause harm or negative consequences beyond the risks encountered in normal life?		
Will the study involve prolonged or repetitive testing?		
Will the study require any deception of participants?		

Figure 4.1 An ethical approval form preliminary checklist.

1. Project title	
2. Location(s) at which project is to be carried out	
3. Background and rationale for study	
4. Aims and objectives of the research and/or the research questions	
5. Methods of data collection *Clearly outline how data will be collected. Copies of questionnaires, interview schedules, or observation guidelines must be appended.*	
6. Recruitment of participants *Give approximate number of participants involved, how they will be identified and invited to participate, and how voluntary, informed consent will be obtained. Information sheets and consent forms must be appended.*	
7. Potential benefits of proposed research *Outline any benefits of the research for: (1) participants involved; (2) yourself as a researcher.*	
8. Steps to be taken to ensure confidentiality of data *Outline steps to ensure confidentiality, privacy and anonymity of data. Research projects must adhere to the requirements of the Data Protection Act.*	

Figure 4.2 Details of your research project.

Name:

Project title:

Background and rationale for study:

_____

_____

Aims and objectives of the research and/or the research questions:

_____

_____

Methods of data collection:

_____

_____

Potential benefits of the proposed research:

_____

_____

How research data will be stored and used:

_____

_____

In undertaking this research project, I understand that individuals may decline to participate and are free to withdraw at any time without giving a reason.

If you would like to ask any questions or make any comments about this research project, please write these below:

_____

_____

_____

_____

Thank you.

Signed:_____Student

Date: _____

Figure 4.3 Research project information sheet.

Name of researcher:

Title of research project:

I consent to the above-named person undertaking a research project in my school.

Signed: _____

Head teacher

Figure 4.4 Research project consent form.

Rigour in action research

Critics of action research often refer to a perceived lack of rigour in studies undertaken. This is not intended, primarily, as a criticism of individual researchers or of the work they have completed; rather it might be seen as a direct attack on the nature of action research itself. So what are the problems to which critics refer and how might action researchers respond to them? To begin with, it has been suggested (Hopkins, 2008, p. 58) that an overuse of words like 'problem', 'improve', 'needs assessment' etc. 'could give the impression that action research is a deficit model of professional development'. In other words, 'Something is wrong, so do this to make it better'.

I agree with Hopkins that action research offers practitioners a powerful tool to enhance their 'professional confidence' (p. 58) and so, with this in mind, it is important to attempt to speak and write about school-based research as positively as we can. However, Wragg (1999, p. 118) distinguishes between two kinds of action research, which he calls 'rational-reactive' and 'intuitive-proactive'. In the first, the researcher examines what is occurring (in a classroom, for example) 'usually with a specific focus on something known to be a problem or in need of improvement, and then draws up a programme to react to, or remediate, what has been discovered' (p. 118). The second type of action research is undertaken by practitioners who know, 'or think they know, what needs to be done, so they implement an intervention programme first, and then visit classrooms to see how well it is progressing' (p. 118). These distinctions are important because they draw attention to different ways of utilising action research to achieve educational goals. It is often the case that particular problems identified within a classroom or school may be tackled effectively through a sharply-focused research study. However, it is important to remember that this is not the only purpose which action research may serve. As Hopkins (2008, p. 58) indicates, it 'provides teachers with a more appropriate alternative to traditional research designs and one that is, in aspiration at least, emancipatory'.

The notion of a 'traditional research design' is an interesting one, not least because action research has frequently been compared unfavourably to it. In attempting to find out why this is the case and whether such a comparison is justifiable, we need to examine relationships between quantitative and qualitative research. Thomas (2009) and Blaxter *et al.* (2001) offer concise explanations of these approaches. According to Thomas (p. 83), 'Quantitative research refers to research using numbers, and qualitative research refers to that which does not use numbers'. Blaxter *et al.* (p. 64) suggest that quantitative research is 'concerned with the collection and analysis of data in numeric form. It tends to emphasise relatively large-scale and representative sets of data'. However, qualitative research 'is concerned with collecting and analysing information in as many forms, chiefly non-numeric, as possible' (p. 64). The authors note that quantitative research is regarded or represented (mistakenly in their view) as attempting to collect 'facts', while qualitative research aims to explore in great detail 'smaller numbers of instances or examples which are seen as being interesting or illuminating, and aims to achieve "depth" rather than "breadth"' (p. 64). Although Dick (2000) suggests that action research is often qualitative in nature, it is possible, as we shall see, for practitioners to use both quantitative and qualitative methods in undertaking their research projects. This is a necessary approach because, as Wragg (1999, p. 10) argues: 'While the counting of events may offer some interesting insights, it falls far short of telling the whole story of classroom life'.

Although acknowledging that there is no 'watertight' distinction between these two approaches, Denscombe (2007, pp. 248–250) suggests that quantitative research tends to be associated with:

- numbers as the unit of analysis;
- analysis;
- large-scale studies;
- a specific focus;
- researcher detachment;
- pre-determined research design.

On the other hand, qualitative research tends to be associated with:

- words as the unit of analysis;
- description;
- small-scale studies;
- an holistic perspective;
- researcher involvement;
- an emergent research design.

Arguments have been advanced against the rigour of action research on the grounds that:

- it is primarily qualitative in nature;
- it is susceptible to 'researcher bias' because practitioners often engage in the study of their own practice;
- it usually involves undertaking small-scale studies (often of a particular classroom or school);
- given the very limited scope of typical action research projects, results obtained from these studies should not be regarded as generalisable beyond their individual contexts.

How might action researchers respond to these criticisms? The best way to begin is by acknowledging that when undertaking research of any kind, it is important that the results deriving from it are sound. Robson (2002 p. 93) discusses how the trustworthiness of research is usually established. In attempting to convince your audiences (and yourself) that your findings are significant, he suggests that you should ask several questions: 'What is it that makes the study believable and trustworthy? What are the kinds of arguments that you can use? What questions should you ask? What criteria are involved?' In offering answers to these questions, Robson refers to several important concepts that are usually associated with 'traditional' research:

- Validity. This is concerned with 'whether the findings are "really" about what they appear to be about' (Robson, 2002, p. 93) or, in Bell's words (2005, p. 117), 'whether an item or instrument measures or describes what it is supposed to measure or describe'.
- Reliability. This refers to 'the consistency or stability of a measure; for example, if it were to be repeated, would the same result be obtained?' (Robson, 2002, p. 93);
- Generalisability. This refers to 'the extent to which the findings of the enquiry are more generally applicable outside the specifics of the situation studied' (Robson, 2002, p. 93).

At this stage, it is important to:

1. determine the extent to which these terms have any applicability to action research;
2. establish how researchers might endeavour to ensure that their studies are as rigorous as possible.

As Robson notes, concepts such as 'validity', 'reliability' and 'generalisability' were initially utilised within the context of traditional 'fixed-design' research, where the aim was to collect quantitative data. Given this, there is a substantial debate as to whether they are applicable to 'flexible-design' research aiming to gather qualitative data (see Chapters 5 and 6 of *Real World Research* (Robson, 2002) for discussions of fixed and flexible designs).

Robson refers to the close relationship that exists between action research and qualitative, flexible-design research, and outlines a number of factors that may lead us plausibly to use the term 'validity' in the context of such investigations. Claiming that a piece of qualitative research 'has validity' is, as Robson (2002, p. 170) rightly suggests, to refer to it as 'being accurate, or correct, or true'. While acknowledging that it is difficult (if not impossible) to verify these characteristics with certainty, he suggests that 'An alternative . . . tack is to focus on the credibility or trustworthiness of the research'. How are these to be determined? Robson refers to a number of strategies for dealing with threats to the validity of a piece of research. These include:

- prolonged involvement in the study (which may take place over weeks or months: 'much longer than is typical in fixed methods research' (Robson, 2002, p. 172);
- triangulation (for example, the use of more than one method of data collection, or more than one observer in the research, or drawing on both quantitative and qualitative approaches);
- negative case analysis ('As you develop theories about what is going on [in your research], you should devote time and attention to searching for instances which will disconfirm your theory' (Robson, 2002, p. 173);
- audit trail (keeping a complete record of your research while carrying it out; this includes raw data such as completed questionnaires, interview transcripts and field notes, audiotapes and videotapes, as well as your research diary or journal – see Robson, 2002, pp. 1–2).

While prolonged involvement in a piece of research may (at least potentially) increase the risk of researcher bias, triangulation, negative case analysis and an effective audit trail may all help to reduce it. Robson also suggests that a researcher's prolonged involvement in a study may help to reduce respondents' bias. This is due to the likely development of a trusting relationship between researcher and respondent, which may decrease the possibility that the latter will provide biased information.

Prolonged involvement, triangulation, negative case analysis, and audit trail are strategies that, if adopted collectively, can reduce substantially possible threats to validity. In this way, the credibility or trustworthiness of the research undertaken is enhanced. In addition, an audit trail offers evidence that you are being careful, systematic and scrupulous about your research. These are important considerations when you are making the case for its reliability.

As regards generalisability, Robson (2002, p. 176) refers to the work of Maxwell (see 1992, 2005) who distinguishes between 'internal' and 'external' generalisability. These refer respectively to the generalisability of conclusions within and outside the setting being researched. As regards the former, unjustifiable selectivity on the part of researchers (for example, in terms of choosing interviewees, or potential respondents to a questionnaire, or particular contexts for observation research) will substantially increase the possibility that their accounts will exhibit bias.

Robson points out that some projects may not seek external generalisability. This is commonly the case with small-scale, funded action research studies, as well as those undertaken within the context of most undergraduate and postgraduate courses. Therefore, it is unwarranted to criticise a piece of research in terms of its lack of generalisability when this is neither a stated goal for the work being conducted, nor an explicit intention of the researcher who carries it out. This is not to deny that small-scale action research has the potential for generalisability. For example, if researchers share details such as the context of and planning for their studies in their reports, readers can explore the relevance of these aspects to their own research. As Macintyre (2000, p. 66) indicates, 'This makes generalisation a much more serious possibility'. For a discussion of bias, reliability, validity and generalisability, within an action research framework, see Macintyre (2000, pp. 48–50 and 66); MacNaughton and Hughes (2009, Chapter 8); and McNiff and Whitehead (2006, Chapter 16).

Dick (1993) details a number of procedures that you may use in order to achieve rigour in your research. These include:

- using multiple sources when collecting data;
- continually testing your assumptions;

- seeking exceptions in cases of apparent agreement and explanations in cases of apparent disagreement;
- being willing to challenge your own ideas.

As regards the latter three points, please remember that these apply both in the context of your general reading and in your fieldwork (or practical research). Mertler (2009, pp. 24–25) also focuses on the theme of 'rigour' in action research and discusses ways in which research projects may be made more rigorous.

Before we move on to discuss examples of action research projects, please consider Reflective Thinking Exercise 4.2.

Reflective Thinking Exercise 4.2

1. What do you consider to be the main criticisms of action research as a mode of enquiry?
2. What can researchers do to counter these criticisms and to ensure that their research projects are as rigorous as possible?

Examples of action research projects

Examining the above issues carefully enables you to develop a solid foundation for your action research project. In order to illustrate how this might be developed, I shall set out three examples using Denscombe's (2007) action research model. In Chapter 1, I suggested that this could be represented in several ways and offered one example (see Figure 1.3 above). I also noted that Hopkins (2008) rightly draws our attention to difficulties which may arise if action research models are offered to practitioners in a prescriptive manner. Given this, I suggest only that the above framework may provide a useful tool with which to undertake an action research project. Its viability will depend entirely on the outcomes of its use in educational settings. Earlier in this chapter, I also referred to Hopkins' concern about a possible overuse of words such as 'problem', 'improve,' etc. With this in mind, I suggest that the word 'problem' in Denscombe's model should be considered as an 'umbrella' term to include the research issue, question, or hypothesis to be examined.

Example 1: Developing an effective school governing body: an action research project

The research project begins with the premise that an effective governing body is essential to the success of a school. Given this, practitioners may be interested to investigate issues such as: how governors' meetings are managed; the agenda items discussed by governors; the length of time taken up by discussions of individual topics; the level of participation by individual governors, etc. This research might be carried out by, for example, undergraduate or postgraduate students; teachers completing funded research projects; and head teachers wishing to find out whether meetings of their schools' governing bodies are being well managed and whether members are participating as fully as possible.

For the purposes of this example, we shall assume that it is the head teacher of a secondary school, Mrs A, who wishes to undertake the project. She has been in post for three years and has attended all meetings of her school's governing body (stage 1: professional practice). Although she usually speaks fully concerning all agenda items, Mrs A has become aware that some members rarely participate in discussions. Furthermore, during her informal conversations with governors, many suggested that meetings were too lengthy and that excessive amounts of time were devoted to administrative matters. When asked why their level of participation was low, some made statements such as:

- 'I am never invited to speak' (student representative).
- 'I find these meetings rather dull and boring' (councillor).
- 'I know very little about many of the topics being discussed' (company director).
- 'Mrs. B usually speaks on behalf of both of us' (parent governor).
- 'I see my role as being to offer support as requested' (staff representative).

Mrs A reflects critically both on her own experience of governors' meetings and the feedback she has received from individual members of the governing body (stage 2: critical reflection). She decides to initiate an action research project with the following aims:

1. To explore the nature and extent of participation in school governors' meetings.
2. To seek the views of members of the governing body about their participation in meetings.
3. To seek the views of members of the governing body about how meetings might be made more effective.
4. To implement change as appropriate (with a view to developing a more effective school governing body).

⇨

After consultation with colleagues from her local education authority and HEI, Mrs A agrees to formalise her research by making an application for a funded research scholarship and receives a grant of £3000. Although not required by the terms of the research to undertake a literature search, she is keen to find out as much information as possible about:

1. school governing bodies;
2. research methodology.

She gains access to her HEI's library database and undertakes several 'key word' searches (e.g. 'school governors'; 'school governing bodies'; 'effective schools'; 'school leadership'; 'educational management') to find important source material (books, journals, Internet websites etc.). Mrs A then visits the website of the Department for Children, Schools and Families (http://www.dcsf.gov.uk) to ascertain whether additional information is available. Under the heading 'School Governors', she finds a website called 'Governornet' (http://governornet.co.uk), which contains some interesting publications. She then moves on to consider some basic texts on research methodology.

While reading a chapter on 'Observation Studies' in Bell's *Doing Your Research Project: A Guide for First-Time Researchers in Education and Social Science* (first edition, 1987, p. 95), Mrs. A finds an observation chart which offers an account of a school governors' meeting, including agenda topics and the extent of individual governors' participation. She decides to adopt this approach as one means of gathering data for her own research study and invites a lecturer from the local HEI to observe the next meeting of the governing body (stage 3: research).

In order to do this (and following Bell's guidance), the lecturer takes some sheets of lined paper and marks each line as representing one minute. Within a generous vertical margin, agenda items and the starting times for their discussion are indicated. Speakers' initials are written in the margin each time they make a contribution to the meeting. Brief notes about the discussions taking place are included on the sheet and a single line is drawn after each agenda item has been completed. A summary sheet, containing the information obtained from the meeting, is then produced.

Mrs A would like the research project to be as rigorous as possible and so decides to supplement the data gathered from the initial observation. She does this in three ways:

1. repeating the observation;
2. developing a questionnaire which is sent to all members of the governing body;
3. interviewing a smaller sample of the group (stage 3: research).

The research instruments used by Mrs A (observation chart, questionnaire and interview schedule) will be discussed in the next chapter.

Example 2: Developing questioning in organisations: an action research project

The research project begins with the premise that it is important for professionals working in a broad range of organisations to develop their questioning skills in order to:

1. improve the quality of their own thinking and practice;
2. improve the quality of colleagues' thinking and practice;
3. enhance the learning and performance of individual groups within organisations;
4. enhance the learning and performance of organisations.

Given this, practitioners may be interested to ask and find answers to the following questions:

- How often do I ask colleagues questions?
- What sort of questions do I ask?
- What can I do to increase the number, range and quality of my questions?
- What can I do to ensure a greater response to questions from my colleagues?

This research might be carried out by undergraduates, postgraduates, and professionals working in organisations. For the purposes of this example, we shall assume that it is a middle manager, Mr B, who works in a retail business and who wishes to undertake the project as part of his study for an MA in Management. He has been in post for eight years and has a broad range of experience within his organisation. He manages a team of 19 staff. At regular meetings, Mr B requests contributions from the group that focus on work undertaken, progress made, issues and problems that arise, etc. Mr B is keen to explore the role his questioning plays in enhancing the group's learning and development (stage 1: professional practice). Having reflected critically on his questioning (stage 2: critical reflection), Mr B considers himself to be someone who asks his colleagues a broad range of questions. He would like to find out whether his own perceptions of his questioning are confirmed through research and so decides to initiate a project with the following aims:

- To ascertain how many questions are asked during a series of meetings covering a range of subjects.
- To ascertain the nature of the questioning that takes place.
- To ascertain which colleagues respond to questions.

⇨

- To ascertain which colleagues do not respond to questions.
- To implement change, as appropriate (focusing on: 'What can I do to increase the number, range and quality of my questions?' and 'What can I do to ensure a greater response from my colleagues to the questions I ask?').

Mr B gains access to his HEI's library database and undertakes two initial 'key word' searches, 'questioning' and 'asking questions'. These produce some interesting insights and areas for additional key word searches. To begin with, Mr B's discovery of a book entitled *The Art of Asking Questions*, dated 1951, indicates that a concern to improve questioning skills is not a recent development. Given this, he decides to discuss, in one of the early chapters of his dissertation, the historical evolution of questioning in professional settings.

Second, his initial searches lead him to explore topics such as 'reflective questioning'; 'the questioning manager'; 'effective questioning skills'; 'questioning and explaining'; and 'questioning and learning'. Further key word searches in these areas enable Mr B to gain access to a broad range of books, journals, Internet websites etc. Finally, he undertakes some initial reading on research methodology.

While reading McGill and Beaty's *Action Learning* (2001), Mr B finds a number of references to questions and questioning. He decides to gather research data using two methods (stage 3: research). The first involves a senior colleague observing his questioning during meetings in order to ascertain the number and nature of the questions asked. Mr B devises an observation chart using a category system that focuses on: open questions; closed questions; affective questions ('How do you feel about . . .?'); probing questions ('What aspects of your behaviour do you think might be relevant here?'); checking questions ('What you plan to do is . . . Is that right?'); and reflective questions ('In what way were your colleague's questions confusing?') (McGill and Beaty, 2001, pp. 128–29).

Mr B wishes to be as rigorous as possible in his research. In order to achieve this, he asks his colleague to observe a series of meetings, not just a single event. He also requests not to be given any feedback after each meeting, so as to ensure that his questioning style remains as consistent as possible. Mr B supplements the data collected in two ways. First, he develops a second observation chart. In its initial form, colleagues' names are written in the left-hand column. Across the top row, numerals indicate the questions asked during a particular period. When Mr B asks a question and receives a response from a colleague, the observer writes 'x' in the appropriate box. Again, this chart is used in several meetings. Second, Mr B catalogues his research by maintaining a personal record of the process. These field notes detail key aspects of the meetings as seen from Mr B's perspective. The observation charts developed in this study will be outlined in the next chapter.

Example 3: Developing thinking skills in the early years classroom: an action research study

The research project begins with the premise that young children should be taught critical thinking, reasoning and argument skills as part of the formal school curriculum. Given this, practitioners may be interested to ask and find answers to the following questions:

- What are 'thinking skills'?
- Do we need to teach thinking skills in schools and, if so, why?
- What obstacles exist which may hinder such teaching?
- How might 'thinking skills' be developed in schools?

This research might be carried out by, for example, undergraduate and postgraduate students, and teachers completing funded research projects. For the purposes of this example, we shall assume that it is a trainee teacher, Ms C, who wishes to undertake the project during her school experience placement. Having attended a conference on the teaching of thinking skills, which was hosted by her HEI during the previous year, she wishes to gain experience of such teaching as quickly as possible (stage 1: professional practice). Having reflected critically on her last school placement (stage 2: critical reflection), where Ms C was able to teach three lessons with a thinking skills focus, and having already completed some basic reading on this topic, she decides to initiate a project with the following aims:

1. To discuss the nature of 'thinking skills'.
2. To argue that thinking skills should be taught in early childhood education.
3. To outline those factors that may inhibit the teaching of thinking skills in early childhood education.
4. To implement a thinking skills programme with a class of 5–6-year-old pupils.

Ms C gains access to her HEI's library database and undertakes several 'key word' searches based on her earlier reading: 'teaching thinking skills'; 'improving reasoning and argument skills', 'education for citizenship', 'personal, social and moral education', 'critical thinking', and 'the cognitive curriculum'. She finds a broad range of books, journals, Internet websites, etc. and undertakes some initial reading on research methodology.

Having read Costello's *Thinking Skills and Early Childhood Education* (2000), Ms C decides to focus on developing young children's moral thinking, through discussing episodes from *Sesame Street* videotapes with a class of 5–6-year-old

⇨

pupils. In order to ensure that her research is as rigorous as possible, she chooses to gather data using two methods (stage 3: research). These are:

1. video taping a lesson taught by her mentor, Mr D;
2. audio taping two of her lessons and transcribing examples of the dialogues in which she engages with her class.

Ms C wishes to explore the processes of argument that children use when speaking. Accordingly, she amends a model of argument (outlined by Costello (2000, pp. 95–96) and presented in the next chapter) and analyses both the videotape and audiotapes with a view to determining the extent to which pupils utilise these processes. Relationships between the collection and analysis of action research data will be examined in Chapter 5.

How Do I Analyse Action Research Data?

Chapter Outline

Analysing research data   66
A model of action research revisited   73
Concluding comments   77

My aims in this chapter are:

- to offer some practical examples of data collection instruments utilised in the three projects mentioned previously;
- to discuss possibilities for data analysis arising from them.

I wish to begin by arguing that there is a close relationship between the collection of action research data and its analysis. In supporting this view, I would refer to my experience of supervising the research projects of students and teachers undertaking a broad range of academic courses, as well as funded research. In all of these cases, practitioners engaged in research are busy individuals: project work is only a small part of what they have to do and so there is a need to use time wisely.

How is this to be achieved? When offering research methodology seminars and modules, I refer to a series of related maxims: 'The better the research instruments we develop to collect data, the more reliable those data will be. The more reliable our data, the greater are our chances of undertaking research that merits the label "rigorous". The more rigorous our research, the more likely it is that our conclusions and recommendations will be significant'.

In the last chapter, I outlined three research projects and suggested methods by which action research data might be collected. Given the length of this book, it is not possible to examine in any depth the particular advantages and possible disadvantages of using questionnaires, interviews, observations etc. within your action research project. However, both Hopkins (2008) and Macintyre (2000) discuss this topic at some length. Also, it should be noted that some authors have devoted entire volumes to discussing themes such as 'developing a questionnaire' (Gillham, 2008a); 'the research interview' (Gillham, 2001, 2005); observation techniques (Gillham, 2008b); and 'case study research methods' (Gillham, 2000). In Chapter 9, I offer a number of suggestions for further reading that will enable you to examine these individual research methods in some detail.

Analysing research data

In considering the analysis of research data, let us begin by looking once again at Example 1, 'Developing an effective school governing body'. As we saw in the previous chapter, the researcher, Mrs A, collects data by utilising three research methods: observation, questionnaire and interview. The first observation produces quantitative data (see Figure 5.1), and these are broadly confirmed by a second observation. The observation chart details the agenda items for the meeting of the school's governing body, the number of minutes for which each member speaks on a particular topic, and the total number of minutes for which members speak expressed as a percentage of the whole. Please consider Reflective Thinking Exercises 5.1 and 5.2.

Reflective Thinking Exercise 5.1

1. How might the data in Figure 5.1 be analysed?
2. What might Mrs A conclude from the data?
3. What is Mrs A entitled to conclude from the data?

Evergreen High School
School Governors' Meeting
1 October, 2010

	Admin (Minutes, etc.)	Curriculum	School inspection	Exams	Discipline	PTA	Staff Development	Other	No.	%
Chair (University lecturer)	++++ ++++		++++ 111	++++ 11	1	1	1	1	29	19.1
Secretary (LEA official)	++++ ++++		111					11	15	9.9
Head teacher	++++	++++ ++++	++++ ++++	++++	111	111	++++	111	44	28.9
Assistant Head teacher	111	111	1111	111				1	14	9.2
Mr P (Councillor)		1111	111		1				8	5.3
Ms L (Councillor)			1					1	2	1.3
Mr E (Company director)		1	11			1			4	2.6
Mrs R (LEA representative)	++++		111	11					10	6.6
Mrs C (Staff representative)		1	11			1	111		7	4.6
Mr J (Student representative)									0	0.0
Mrs B (Parent governor)	11	111	11	111	1	++++		11	18	11.8
Mr Y (Parent governor)						1			1	0.7
Total time (in minutes)	35	22	38	20	6	12	9	10	152	100

Figure 5.1 Observation chart.

Reflective Thinking Exercise 5.2

Having examined the observation chart, consider the six statements below. Do you agree with them? If yes, why? If no, why not?

1. Mr J [student representative] did not speak during the meeting.
2. Contributions made by the head teacher and chairperson take up almost half the meeting.
3. Some members contribute very little to the meeting, especially Ms L [councillor], Mr E [company director], Mr Y [parent governor] and Mr J [student representative].
4. The school does not have any problems with pupils' discipline.
5. The school's inspection report was either very good or very poor.
6. The head teacher and assistant head teacher work closely together and are mutually supportive.

A number of additional statements might be added to the above list and it is instructive to consider exactly what might or might not be concluded justifiably from such an observation chart, as well as what remains an hypothesis to be investigated further. For example, it is unjustifiable to conclude from the chart alone that 'Mr J [student representative] did not speak during the meeting'. As one of my students pointed out:

1. Mr J may have spoken for less than one minute on all agenda items;
2. a concise but effective contribution to a discussion might be (and often is) made in less than one minute.

While collecting quantitative data may make an important contribution to an action research project, it should be remembered that information represented in an observation chart needs to be interpreted in exactly the same way as other data gathered during a research study. The so-called 'facts' that emerge from quantitative research never speak for themselves: they have to be supported by reasons, evidence, and argument. The importance of Figure 5.1 is that it provides us with a number of questions to pursue via other research methods, such as the questionnaire and interview schedule developed by Mrs A. Let us look at each in turn, beginning with the questionnaire (see Figure 5.2).

1. For how many years have you been a member of the school's governing body?

< 1 year ☐   1 year ☐   2 years ☐

3 years ☐   4 years ☐   5 years ☐

> 5 years ☐

2. Which of the following statements best describes your <u>attendance</u> at governors' meetings?

I attend all meetings ☐

I attend most meetings ☐

I attend some meetings ☐

I rarely attend meetings ☐

Comments _____

_____

_____

3. Which of the following statements best describes your <u>participation</u> in governors' meetings?

I always contribute to discussions ☐

I often contribute to discussions ☐

I sometimes contribute to discussions ☐

I rarely contribute to discussions ☐

I never contribute to discussions ☐

Comments _____

_____

_____

Figure 5.2 Questionnaire.

4. Have you contributed to the discussion of the following topics?

Administrative matters	Yes ☐	No ☐
Curriculum	Yes ☐	No ☐
School inspection	Yes ☐	No ☐
Examinations	Yes ☐	No ☐
Discipline	Yes ☐	No ☐
Parent Teacher Association	Yes ☐	No ☐
Staff development	Yes ☐	No ☐
Other	Yes ☐	No ☐

If 'Other', please state topic(s) _____

_____

_____

5. Would you like to make a greater contribution to governors' meetings?

Yes ☐   No ☐

6. If 'Yes', please indicate any factors that may inhibit your increasing participation:

_____

_____

_____

Figure 5.2 *Continued.*

7. How would you describe the management of governors' meetings?

Excellent ☐   Good ☐

Satisfactory ☐   Less than adequate ☐

Poor ☐   Don't know ☐

Comments _____

_____

_____

8. Do you have any suggestions concerning how governors' meetings might be improved?

Yes ☐   No ☐

Comments _____

_____

_____

9. Is the governing body successful in fulfilling its aims?

Very ☐   Quite ☐   Not really ☐

Not at all ☐   Don't know ☐

Comments _____

_____

_____

Figure 5.2 *Continued.*

---

10. Do you have any suggestions concerning how the governing body might become more successful in fulfilling its aims?

Comments _____

_____

_____

Figure 5.2 *Continued.*

Mrs A has piloted the above questionnaire carefully, i.e. she has produced a draft version, circulated it for comment to two colleagues, and then made several amendments as a result of responses received. She is aware of the need to pilot all data-gathering instruments, in order to ascertain the amount of time recipients take to complete them, to ensure that all the questions and accompanying instructions are outlined clearly and to enable items to be removed or amended as necessary (Bell, 2005).

Mrs A aims to collect both quantitative and qualitative datas. As regards the former, she provides a variety of possible options for response. In question two, four alternatives are offered; in question three, there are five to consider and so on. This reduces the possibility that respondents may reply automatically to questions, or persist in choosing the middle option in a non-reflective manner. On several occasions, Mrs A offers respondents the opportunity to write comments. These will be analysed individually to determine whether common or uncommon themes emerge. In analysing action research data, Macintyre (2000, p. 91) offers a concise explanation of four key terms: *themes* ('the consistent ideas which emerged'); *incidence* ('how often something occurred, or the number of questionnaire replies which said the same thing'); *patterns* ('the timing of the occurrences – whether they were single or in a cluster'); and *trends* ('the frequency of the patterns'). These enable researchers to offer explanations for what has taken place, rather than just descriptions of events. This schema will be useful in analysing data that emerge from Mrs A's interview schedule, which contains the following questions:

- Why did you become a member of the school's governing body?
- Have you found being a member of the governing body a worthwhile experience?
- Have you found being a member of the governing body an enjoyable experience?

- As a member of the governing body, what would you like it to achieve?
- Are you able to attend meetings of the governing body regularly? If not; why not?
- How might you contribute to the success of the governing body?
- Describe some characteristics of a successful governing body.
- Are these characteristics evident in the governing body of which you are a member?
- Describe some characteristics of a well-managed governors' meeting.
- Are these characteristics evident in the meetings of the governing body that you attend?
- Do you leave governors' meetings feeling that you have said everything that you wanted to say? If not, why not?
- About which agenda items do you tend to contribute to discussions? Why?
- About which agenda items do you tend not to contribute to discussions? Why not?
- How, if at all, might you make a greater contribution to governors' meetings?
- Could you say something about factors, if any that may inhibit you making a greater contribution to meetings?
- What assistance, if any, do you need in order to make a greater contribution to meetings?
- Who might offer you such assistance?
- Do you have any views about how, if at all, governors' meetings might be improved?
- Do you have any views about how, if at all, the governing body might become more effective?

Reflective Thinking Exercise 5.3 focuses on the development and discussion of a draft questionnaire and interview schedule.

Reflective Thinking Exercise 5.3

1. Write a draft questionnaire related to your proposed research topic.
2. Write a draft interview schedule related to your proposed research topic.

Discuss these with your tutor and make amendments as necessary.

A model of action research revisited

Having analysed the research data, Mrs A is now able to translate her findings into an action plan (stage 4 of Denscombe's (2007) action research model: strategic planning). For example, this might involve the development of strategies to encourage greater participation in governors' meetings, for example, asking members to speak to individual agenda items; modifying the agenda to ensure that all governors have at least one topic concerning which they could make a contribution to discussions; introducing seminars to develop governors' knowledge of particular issues etc. Once these strategies have been implemented (stage 5: action), they will have an impact on professional practice (stage 1) and so the action research cycle begins again. After a period of time, Mrs A engages in further critical reflection to determine the effectiveness of her action (stage 2: evaluate changes). At this point, the research may come to an end, or further research may be required. If the latter is the case, then Mrs A returns to stage 3 of the cycle and engages in another round of systematic and rigorous enquiry.

This format may be repeated in the other two projects outlined in the last chapter. Before commencing your own action research study, it would be beneficial to re-visit the second of these examples and to discuss ways in which stages 4 and 5 of Denscombe's (2007) cycle might be reached. To assist you in this, following are the two observation charts (the first uses a category system) that were devised by Mr B during his project on 'Developing questioning in organisations' (see Figures 5.3 and 5.4).

Please consider the question outlined in Reflective Thinking Exercise 5.4.

Reflective Thinking Exercise 5.4

1. How might you analyse the data provided in the observation charts below to develop an action plan and instigate change within the group?

1.	Manager asks open questions	/ / / / / / / / / /
2.	Manager asks closed questions	/ /
3.	Manager asks affective questions	/ / / / / / /
4.	Manager asks probing questions	/ / /
5.	Manager asks checking questions	/ / / / / / / / / / / / / /
6.	Manager asks reflective questions	/ / /

Figure 5.3 Observation chart 1.

	Q1	Q2	Q3	Q4	Q5	Q6	Q7	Q8	Q9	Q10	Q11	Q12	Q13	Q14	Q15	Q16	Q17	Q18	Q19
A																			×
B	×												×						
C														×					
D		×																	
E																			
F															×				
G			×	×	×					×	×	×							
H						×													
I										×									
J																			
K					×											×	×	×	
L								×	×										
M							×			×									×
N																			
O										×									
P										×									
Q															×				
R											×								
S		×																	

Figure 5.4 Observation chart 2.

Assessing Progress in Argument

Processes of Argument

The pupil is able to:

    express a point clearly;

    take a point of view, express an opinion;

    make a personal value statement;

    express a preference;

    give an example;

    give several examples;

    give appropriate examples;

    make a comparison;

    give a reason;

    give a variety of reasons;

    give appropriate reasons;

    quote evidence;

    weigh up evidence;

    refer to own experience to support arguments;

    listen and respond to others' points of view.

Figure 5.5 A model of argument.

Finally, we turn to the third research project, undertaken by Ms C, entitled 'Developing thinking skills in the early years classroom'. Figure 5.5 outlines the amended model of argument she uses when introducing a thinking skills programme to develop young children's moral thinking.

Having collected research data by means of audio recording and video recording, how should Ms C proceed with the task of analysis? The best way to begin is to examine the videotape of her mentor's lesson and to write down the names of children who demonstrate any of the above processes of argument, together with the statement they make and the process that is involved. For example: 'Mary – gives a reason – 'Because it would be cruel to animals'.

This raw data can be transferred to a second sheet, where pupils' contributions or examples of particular processes could be grouped. This will enable Ms C to determine which pupils are demonstrating competence in regard to specific processes. If the argument model was used in a number of different lessons, it would be possible to indicate pupils' progress over time and to alter teaching strategies accordingly. Once Ms C has completed the analysis of the videotape, she can begin to analyse the audiotapes of her two lessons (and perhaps compare her results to those achieved by her mentor). For a fuller account of the processes involved in analysing data from videotapes and pupils' dialogues, see Costello (2000). In addition, Macintyre (2000) discusses a number of strategies for recording research findings (see also 'audiotape recording/videotape recording' in Chapter 9).

Concluding comments

In concluding this chapter, please note the following points regarding data analysis. All the data you collect should be discussed in your project report. If you are unable to analyse all of the information you have obtained, the reasons for your selection of particular data should be made clear. Remember that it is possible to display your results in a variety of ways (e.g. observation charts, pie-charts, bar graphs etc.). Finally, use appendices to offer the reader a more extensive account of your research than is permitted within individual chapters. For example, if you discuss brief passages from a dialogue with pupils in the main body of the text, you might wish to provide a more substantial extract in an appendix (see Macintyre, 2000).

In Chapter 2, I referred to a number of problems that have been raised in the context of educational research. Wragg (1999, p. 108) notes that cynicism about the aims of such research and its impact on practice is evident even among teachers. However, he argues that classroom observation research 'can make a significant contribution to the improvement of teaching competence, especially if teachers and schools, as a matter of policy, research their own practice and act on their findings'.

How Do I Produce an Action Research Report? 6

Chapter Outline

Requirements and guidelines for writing action research reports   79

Once you have collected and analysed your action research data, you are ready to produce a report of your findings. In doing this, it is useful to consider two preliminary questions:

- For whom are you writing the report?
- What are the particular requirements or guidelines for writing the report?

If you are undertaking an action research project as part of a course of study for an academic qualification, your audience will include your tutor and (potentially) an external examiner. Completed projects are usually retained by your HEI, so that they may be read by those undertaking future research projects. Given this, it is important to remember, when writing, that your work will also be read by other practitioners. If you are undertaking funded research (not necessarily, for an academic qualification), your audience will include both the funding body and other practitioners.

Requirements and guidelines for writing action research reports

Usually, there are specific requirements or guidelines for writing the action research report. Before beginning to write, consider these carefully. These requirements include a word limit for the project. You may also be given guidelines concerning the presentation of the project report. Here is one example:

- Paper size: A4.
- Your project must be word-processed using Times or Times New Roman 12 point.
- Margins: left-hand – 3 cm; right-hand – 2 cm; top – 3 cm; bottom – 2 cm.
- All pages should be numbered.
- Use double spacing throughout.
- Either spiral ring binding or soft binding for initial submission and hard binding after examination.

As regards the format of reports, I shall outline examples taken from: (1) an undergraduate/postgraduate project; (2) a funded research project (see Figures 6.1 and 6.2).

As Example 1 indicates, the structures of undergraduate and postgraduate project reports tend to be very similar (and are often identical). The basic differences between the two reports are:

1. the word limit stipulated for each;
2. the levels of critical reflection and analysis required in writing them;
3. the breadth and depth of research being discussed.

Example 1

- Front cover to include title of research project; candidate's name; degree title; date of submission.
- Contents page.
- Declaration.
- Summary.
- Acknowledgements.
- Introduction.
- Chapters.
- Appendices.
- Bibliography.

Figure 6.1 Format for an undergraduate / postgraduate research project report.

Example 2

- Front cover to include funding body; title of award (e.g. 'Teacher Research Scholarship'); title of project; candidate's name; interim or final report; date of submission.
- Summary of the report.
- An outline of the aims of the research.
- Methodology.
- A summary of the results (a complete set of results should be included in the appendices).
- Conclusions from the research, including recommendations.
- Evaluation of the process.

(See GTCW, 2002b, pp. 15–17)

Figure 6.2 Format for a funded research project report.

Action research reports: a possible format

It is useful to consider the format of a typical report:

Contents page Here you should list chapter and other headings in the order in which they are presented in the report. Remember to include the page number on which chapters, etc. begin.

Declaration A brief statement to indicate that the project submitted offers an account of your own independent research. Typically, you may be asked to sign a statement such as: 'I certify that the whole of this work is the result of my individual effort, and that all quotations from books, journals etc., have been acknowledged'.

Summary A brief synopsis of the project (usually no more than a few hundred words). You should write this once you have completed the rest of the report. The summary draws attention to the key aspects of each of your chapters. You may wish to make reference to your project's aims, its theoretical underpinning, the approach to the research which you have adopted (e.g. action research), research methods used to collect data, results of the research, conclusions and recommendations for future practice; and implications for your own professional development.

Acknowledgements Here you need to thank those people who have assisted you in the completion of your project: your tutor or mentor; teachers and pupils with whom you have worked; those who responded to your questionnaire or who agreed to be interviewed by you etc. It is also possible to mention family members or others who have helped you, but please remember that the overall statement should be concise and to the point. Schools, teachers and pupils should not be identified by name, as it is an accepted convention of research that anonymity should be preserved. If you are unsure about this, please consult your tutor or mentor. A typical sentence might begin: 'I should like to thank the staff and pupils at the primary school where I undertook my research for ...'

Introduction Like the summary, this details the key aspects of your project but at greater length. Here, your aim is to outline the nature of the project as a whole. This is followed by a brief but systematic examination of the central themes of your individual chapters. You may also wish to refer to the contents of your appendices. When writing your report, it is useful to consider it in terms of a 'journey' on which you are embarking. Remember, too, that whoever reads your work (tutors, mentors, external examiners, or other practitioners) will 'travel' with you in their turn. With this in mind, write the introduction in such a way that it offers an account of the important 'staging posts' of your 'journey': why or how you became interested in the topic being researched; how you developed its precise focus and the project's aims; how your review of the literature developed your knowledge of the topic and influenced your practical research; and how you undertook the research and analysed data emerging from it. Finally, you should refer to the conclusions you draw from your work, as well as to possible recommendations for future practice. The implications of the research for your own professional development should also be indicated. Because the introduction should offer an accurate account of your research project, you should write it immediately before the summary (which may be derived from it).

Chapters These constitute the main part of your report. The requirements or guidelines for your project may specify the number of chapters your report should contain (they may even extend to providing you with chapter titles, for example, 'Review of the Literature', 'Research Context', 'Research Methods' etc.). On the other hand, you may simply be asked to set your work out in terms of the reading you have undertaken (which should provide a theoretical underpinning for your study) and the practical research you have completed. In the latter case, it is important for you to develop your own structure for the project and I offer an example of this below. Essentially chapters should provide:

1. a critical review of the relevant literature;
2. information about the nature and context of your research (including methods of data collection and analysis);
3. a discussion of the results of your research;
4. conclusions and recommendations.

Appendices These contain material to which you have referred in the main body of the text, such as: examples of children's work; blank questionnaire, interview and observation schedules; research ethics documentation; extended versions of audiotape or videotape transcripts; charts, tables, diagrams, etc.

Bibliography This contains full references to all sources (books, chapters in edited books, journal articles, Internet websites etc.) to which you have referred in the text (either by means of quotation or citation – see below for a discussion of these). Once again, the requirements or guidelines for your research project may indicate a preferred style of presentation for the bibliography. If this is not the case, the bibliography at the end of this book utilises a format that you may wish to adopt.

Following is an example of a possible structure for a project report. In developing it, I have chosen the third research project discussed in Chapters 4 and 5:

Title
Developing Thinking Skills in the Early Years Classroom: An Action Research Study.

Introduction
Outlines, chapter by chapter, the contents and main arguments/conclusions of the project.

Chapter 1: Preliminary issues to be discussed
Introduction sets out the aims and scope of this chapter. Chapter examines important preliminary questions: What are 'thinking skills'? Do we need to teach thinking skills in schools and, if so, why? What obstacles exist that may hinder such teaching (e.g. the problem of indoctrination in schools)? Summary of chapter.

Chapter 2: Critical review of the literature

Introduction sets out the aims and scope of this chapter. Chapter offers a critical evaluation of some of the literature on the teaching of thinking skills and examines the work of selected educators who are prominent in this field. Answers questions such as: are thinking skills being taught in primary schools? How? Is this enough? Summary of chapter.

Chapter 3: The research project

Introduction to the chapter sets out the aims and objectives of your research project: teaching thinking skills to a class of 5–6-year-old pupils. Chapter details the research issue/question/problem/hypothesis to be examined and the timescale for the study, and describes the educational setting for the project (e.g. school and classroom etc.). Discusses why action research has been selected as the mode of enquiry or investigation, describes the research tools used (video taping; audio taping) and states how you selected and analysed action research data. Summary of chapter.

Chapter 4: Results of the research

Introduction sets out the aims and scope of this chapter. Chapter details the results of your research project and examines critically some of the data produced (dialogues with pupils). Results of the research are to be explained and evaluated. Summary of chapter.

Chapter 5: Conclusions and recommendations

Introduction sets out the aims and scope of this chapter. Chapter outlines a summary of the project, linking results of the research to earlier chapters and offering some conclusions. Recommendations for the improvement of educational practice and implications for the researcher's professional development should be outlined.

Please consider the following points when writing your research report. You should demonstrate continuity and progression throughout the text, so that it reads as a coherent and developing narrative. The best way to do this is to make explicit connections between chapters. For example, Chapter 1 of this book concludes as follows: 'Having examined the question "What is action research?" arguments for undertaking it in educational settings will be explored in the next chapter'.

You may be asked to write your report in the first person ('I would argue . . .') or third person ('It is argued . . .'). Sometimes tutors or mentors have a preference for one of these approaches. Before you begin your report, be sure that you know how your tutor or mentor would like it to be written.

Remember to avoid plagiarism (Neville, 2010). According to Webster's Collegiate Dictionary, to plagiarise means 'to steal or purloin and pass off as one's own the ideas, words, writings etc. of another'. This may be a deliberate act or undertaken unintentionally. The best way to avoid plagiarism is to ensure that, when quoting from a source such as a book or journal article, you acknowledge the source by using speech marks and providing a full reference in the text. In order to illustrate how this is done, I have provided many examples of quoting from the work of others throughout the book.

Use both quotation and citation to illustrate your own developing arguments. One way to cite another's work is to summarise it in your own words. Another approach is to refer to particular sources as examples to illustrate the point you are making. For example, you might write as follows: 'I would argue that action research aims to improve professional practice (Macintyre, 2000; Hopkins, 2008). This is because . . .' Again, I have incorporated examples of citation in this book.

Offer an honest account of your research project. Do not attempt to disguise the problems that you may have experienced with it, or the fact that you have been unable (due to circumstances beyond your control) to fulfil all the aims with which you began. For example, it is possible that, having intended for your project to take place over eight weeks, you had to complete it in four weeks. If this is the case, say so in your report and discuss the consequences of the reduced timescale for your research. Did you need to amend your aims? Were there fewer opportunities to collect data? How did you respond to the situation? What data were you able to gather? How did you analyse the data? Can you offer conclusions and recommendations on the basis of the work that you were able to complete? Remember that there is no such thing as a 'perfect' research project. All that a tutor, mentor or external examiner can expect from you is that you have:

1. done your best to think carefully about the development of your project;
2. devised an appropriate project proposal, including a viable set of aims;
3. reviewed the relevant literature as appropriate;

4. attempted to ensure rigour in the research you have carried out; and
5. written an accurate account of your work, with appropriate conclusions and recommendations.

Before submitting your report, or portions of it (even in draft form) to your tutor or mentor, ensure that you have removed spelling, typographical and other errors from the text. Then ask someone else (perhaps a colleague within your institution or another member of your course) to read and comment on it. This will provide additional feedback about your work and increase its potential for rigour. Finally, retain a paper copy of your report and also keep a copy on a USB memory stick and/or on the hard drive of your computer.

Reflective Thinking Exercise 6.1 focuses on writing and discussing the draft introduction to and summary of your research report.

Reflective Thinking Exercise 6.1

1. Write a draft Introduction to your research report.
2. Write a draft Summary of your research report.

Discuss the Introduction and Summary with your tutor or mentor and make necessary amendments.

How Will My Action Research Report be Assessed?

7

Chapter Outline

A model of assessing progress in argument in higher education   88

Students' views of assessment   91

Assessing research projects: some examples   93

My aims in this chapter are to discuss assessment in higher education and to offer examples of possible ways in which your action research project may be assessed. In particular, the following will be explored:

- a model of assessing progress in argument in higher education;
- students' views of assessment;
- assessing research projects.

There is now a substantial literature on assessment in higher education. Much of this has focused on issues such as: assessment and student learning (Gibbs and Dunbat-Goddet, 2007); providing assessment feedback to students on the work they have submitted (Mutch, 2003; Oxford Learning Institute (undated); Rae and Cochrane, 2008) and students' use of that feedback (Pitts, 2005). Two important themes are: (1) the need to prepare students adequately to undertake a broad range of assignments (including research projects) by sharing with them the criteria by which such work will be assessed; (2) the importance of students' participation in discussions about the assessment process, both before and after this has taken place.

A model of assessing progress in argument in higher education

In the Introduction to this book, I referred to the importance of developing students' critical thinking, reasoning and argument skills. Elsewhere (Costello, 2007b), I have discussed a model of assessing progress in argument which was developed as a result of undertaking collaborative teaching and assessment with a colleague, Rob Norris. Having provided some seminars as part of a final year undergraduate module, we set an examination and agreed that we would each mark half of the students' work.

On examining the scripts assessed by Norris, I saw that he had treated written answers as though they were longer, word-processed assignments. In all cases, the text was closely annotated with comments indicating where, in the view of the marker; students had been more or less successful in terms of what they had written. Having scrutinised the examination scripts, it was clear to me that my colleague had utilised his own *implicit* model of argument (in contrast to the *explicit* model which was discussed, in the context of Ms C's action research project, in Chapters 4 and 5). In order to assess the former in greater depth, I wrote out all the comments made by Norris on the scripts and grouped them under the headings 'Plus Points' and 'Minus Points' (see Figure 7.1). The 'forward slash' symbols indicate the number of times that Norris found these points in the students' work.

From an examination of the model, it is evident that it offers a clear and concise framework by which students' progress in developing the skills of argument may be assessed. However, this model represents the critical reflection of a single individual. In order to foster students' thinking, reasoning and argument skills, I would suggest that certain prerequisites are necessary. To begin with, academic tutors need to discuss, debate and ultimately agree on appropriate models for assessing these skills (for a discussion of thinking skills frameworks, see Moseley *et al.* 2005). Second, these models should be shared and discussed with students *in advance* of formal assessments taking place. Finally, at the conclusion of the assessment process, tutors should encourage students to evaluate their academic performance critically, as a basis for agreeing short-, medium- and long-term goals for future work. I would argue that students' full involvement in the assessment process is a necessary condition for the improvement of their academic performance.

Plus Points

Straight into the question/to the point //
Sticks closely to the task of answering the question //
Sense of immediacy in answer/sense of debate /
Deals directly and crisply with key developments in policy ///
Clear/economical/well-paced/well-expressed/well-structured argument ////////////
Critical thinking/analysis/argument/evaluation/personal critical voice ///////
Grasp of complexity of issues/attitudes ////
Evaluates approaches /
Raises interesting questions /
Concepts/issues grasped/identified/clarified ////
Identifies development of policies/their characteristics/key problems ///
Demonstrates some awareness of issues /
Describes context with some reference to issues /
Shows understanding/awareness of historical developments and key issues/concepts ///
Substantial/good reference to journal and other literature ///
Refers to/some substantiation from literature /////
Some referencing /
Cites evidence /////
Gives/lists reasons //
Has the key ideas /
Sound argument //
Relevant statements/arguments //
Some relevant points /
Keeps argument going /

Minus Points

Does not get straight into/to grips with question //
Answer runs in parallel with the question rather than addressing it directly /
Quote is not sufficiently well-addressed /
Lacks clarity of conceptualisation /
Provides references to support argument but simplistic at times /
Not so good in citing research evidence /
Tends to lack substantial evidence /
Weak on reference and evidence //
Only some referencing /
Some reference to literature but not to research /
No evidence of reading //

Figure 7.1 A model of assessing progress in argument in higher education.

Not well-informed /
Lacks clear thread of argument /
Points not welded together into an argument /
Grapples with key concepts/arguments but with some lack of control /
Does not marshal arguments for and against sufficiently well /
Shaky/inadequate grasp of key concepts //
Does not demonstrate clear understanding through analysis/evaluation /
Gives examples rather than analyses issues /
Rushed argument with little critical analysis /
Demonstrates lack of knowledge of research /
Identifies issues around the question /
Gaps in content /
Repetitious /
Reader left to make connections /
Argument at level of invective /
Catalogue of bold and unsubstantiated assertions /
High on assertion /
Low on analysis/evaluation ////
Lacks analysis/evidence /
Answer not structured /
Answer poorly structured /
Answers at a common sense level ///
Naïve and over-simplified ///
Largely misses point of the question /
No depth /
No references //
Poor expression //
Plan looks better than essay /

Figure 7.1 *Continued.*

Reflective Thinking Exercise 7.1 invites you to consider the model of assessing progress in argument in higher education.

Reflective Thinking Exercise 7.1

1. What can you learn from Figure 7.1 in order to improve your research project?
2. Look carefully at the 'Plus Points' and 'Minus Points'. Do you want to add anything to these lists? Why/why not?

Students' views of assessment

One way to encourage students' reflective thinking about the assessment process is to ascertain their views about the more general issue of studying in higher education. Currently, I am engaged in a research project that aims to explore keys issues concerning teaching, learning and assessment across three years of an undergraduate degree. Phase one of the project has focused on induction into higher education and I have asked two cohorts of first-year students, who are undertaking an undergraduate degree in Education, a number of questions (Costello, 2009a). Some of these are set out below, together with examples of students' responses (see Figure 7.2).

How can students' best be prepared to undertake study in higher education?	How can lecturers help to facilitate students' academic success?
Students should be mentally and physically prepared and focused to put everything into the course and must take responsibility for their own learning. Students must be committed to the degree programme in order to gain maximum knowledge and understanding from lectures. Study hard and attend all lectures. Take any opportunity available to gain help or information from those who offer it. Study skills are invaluable, especially as a mature student returning to education after twenty years. To know what is expected of us when writing assignments. Have help with assignment writing, such as how to structure an essay and how to write references. Open days to prepare students and allow them to see if higher education is for them.	Help with assignment layout and discuss assignment title words. Give clear explanation of the content of the assignment and of assessment criteria in order to dispel any confusion. Ensure feedback is given after every assignment on a one-to-one basis. Make time for students' questions, so students know areas which need improvement and can develop these areas for future assignments. Offer critical advice on assignments. It's good to be positive but we cannot improve without being given advice on what we have done wrong.
Considering tutors' feedback on assignments you have completed in year 1, write down three things you have done well.	*Considering tutors' feedback on assignments you have completed in year 1, write down three aspects of your work that require further improvement.*
Knowledge and understanding of subject area. Analysed question well. Researched well for assignments. Good range of sources – articles, books and websites.	Ensure I understand the question completely. Ensuring that I meet the expectations of the marking tutor through the assessment criteria. Introduction to assignment is too brief.

Figure 7.2 Questionnaire for students in higher education.

Evidence of good planning.	Write more detailed conclusions.
Quotations selected appropriately.	Justify quotations.
Clearly set out and well structured.	Sometimes points made are a bit disjointed.
Written fluently to engage the reader.	Present bibliography in an appropriate manner.
Gave good ideas for developing oral skills with effective examples.	Proofreading needs attention.
Made better use of references.	Issues with spelling, punctuation and common grammatical errors.
Good presentation.	Adhere to word limit.
Critical argument.	Develop argument skills.
Essay reflects the effort I put into the work.	Supporting arguments with relevant evidence.
	Use a broader range of source material to support my arguments.
	Try to make arguments more succinct.
What academic support do you require to make these improvements?	*What can you do to facilitate your own success?*
More guidance about assignment writing.	Ask if I am unsure about the essay that has been set.
Examples of good assignments, good layout and presentation to be made available.	Start the assignment as early as possible.
Learning thinking, reasoning and argument skills.	Research topic in greater depth.
More study skills lectures – how arguments are to be focused and refined.	Plan my assignments in line with the marking criteria.
One-to-one support where an individual feels they would benefit from it.	Spend more time on the assignments.
Critical feedback.	Do more reading on assignments and read more in between assignments to build up my knowledge.
Open lectures where lecturers are free to answer any questions we may have.	Practise my essay writing.
	Remember to analyse my quotes in depth.
	Improve my reasoning and argument skills.
	Read more books, study harder, listen to other people's judgements and liaise better with lecturers.
	Accept positive, constructive feedback and criticism.
	Discuss my assignments with tutors so I can get the feedback needed to do better next time.
	Continue with the standard of work I have produced during year one and develop my style of academic writing further.

Figure 7.2 *Continued.*

Many of the comments made by my students bear directly on the issue of assessment. For example, this is evident from their responses concerning tutors' assessment feedback, as well as to the question 'How can lecturers help to facilitate students' academic success?' Reflective Thinking Exercise 7.2 focuses on your own analysis of the students' comments outlined above, while Reflective Thinking Exercise 7.3 is concerned with tutors' assessment of your assignments.

Reflective Thinking Exercise 7.2

1. Which of the students' comments in Figure 7.2 relate particularly to the assessment of their work?
2. What can you learn from these comments in order to improve the quality of your research project?
3. Do you have any questions for your tutor?

Reflective Thinking Exercise 7.3

1. Look carefully at your tutors' assessment of the assignments you have already completed.
2. What can you learn from the tutors' comments in order to improve the quality of your research project?

Assessing research projects: some examples

At this stage, it will be useful to consider some typical examples of how your research project may be assessed. Following are several assessment pro formas that focus on undergraduate and postgraduate projects. These are as follows: (1) two undergraduate pro formas that focus on a broad range of attainment (40–80/100 marks); (2) a postgraduate pro forma; (3) a postgraduate dissertation pro forma. Please note that your research project may be assessed by more than one tutor and that your mark (or grade) will need to be confirmed by an examiner who is external to your HEI.

Undergraduate Research Project: Example 1

Assignment Title: **Developing Effective Approaches to Education for Citizenship in the Primary School: An Action Research Study.**

Assessment Criteria	Mark
Evidence of research and scholarly activity to inform practice: *Books, journal articles and appropriate websites concerned with action research and education for citizenship.*	9/10
Evidence of critical thinking, analysis and argument: *Using relevant documentation to develop your arguments about the nature, purposes and practice of action research and education for citizenship.*	7/10
Clarity of focus: *Rationale for undertaking action research in schools or other professional settings.*	8/10
Undertaking a small-scale research project: *Outline your action research study.*	40/50
Reflection on the quality of your own professional learning in relation to future practice: *What are the implications of your action research study both for pupils' learning and your own teaching?*	8/10
Clarity of written expression: *Use of sub-headings to structure your work; correct grammar and punctuation; assignment written within the word limit.*	4/5
Presentation: *All references acknowledged; work word-processed and presented appropriately.*	4/5

Marking Tutor's Comments

This is an excellent piece of work, into which it is clear that you have put a great deal of effort. You have:

- drawn upon an excellent range of sources to support your arguments;
- established a clear focus for the assignment;
- completed a very good action research project;
- offered several examples which demonstrate the link between educational theory and practice;
- expressed your own professional learning by outlining the implications of your research study;
- offered appropriate conclusions and recommendations for practice.
- included the required research ethics documentation in your appendices.

In reflecting on your assignment, consider the following questions:

- How would you respond to the view that education for citizenship is essentially an exercise in indoctrination?
- Have you offered an adequate justification for the action research model used to develop your research project?

The assignment has an appropriate structure and, overall, there is a very good standard of presentation. Please see my comments in the text. Well done!

Recommended Mark: 80
Marking Tutor:
Tutor's Signature:
Date:

Undergraduate Research Project: Example 2

Assignment Title: **Developing Effective Approaches to Education for Citizenship in the Primary School: An Action Research Study.**

Assessment Criteria	Mark
Evidence of research and scholarly activity to inform practice: *Books, journal articles and appropriate websites concerned with action research and education for citizenship.*	5/10
Evidence of critical thinking, analysis and argument: *Using relevant documentation to develop your arguments about the nature, purposes and practice of action research and education for citizenship.*	3/10
Clarity of focus: *Rationale for undertaking action research in schools or other professional settings.*	5/10
Undertaking a small-scale research project: *Outline your action research study.*	22/50
Reflection on the quality of your own professional learning in relation to future practice: *What are the implications of your action research study both for pupils' learning and your own teaching?*	3/10
Clarity of written expression: *Use of sub-headings to structure your work; correct grammar and punctuation; assignment written within the word limit.*	1/5
Presentation: *All references acknowledged; work word-processed and presented appropriately.*	1/5

Marking Tutor's Comments

You have used some appropriate sources to support your action research study but your text is much too descriptive (to the exclusion of analysis and evaluation). There is some very limited evidence of critical thinking, analysis and argument, and you attempt to establish a relationship between educational theory and practice. You offer some reflections on what you have learned from undertaking the research project. Your mode of presentation requires attention throughout. Please see my comments in the text, particularly concerning clarity of written expression. In considering your assignment, ask yourself the following questions:

- What is action research?
- Why are you using action research to explore education for citizenship in the primary school?
- Have you clarified the purposes of education for citizenship?
- Why have you chosen to collect research data using only a very brief questionnaire?
- Have you analysed your research data fully, rather than leaving the reader to interpret them?

Recommended Mark: 40

Marking Tutor:

Tutor's Signature:

Date:

Postgraduate Research Project

Assignment Title:

Part 1: 3000 words

Identify an action research topic and analyse the key issues that would form the basis of it.

Part 2: 3000 words

Outline the action research design, its implementation and evaluation.

Content:

This assignment offers a critical evaluation of the role of play in early childhood settings. You begin by offering a thorough introduction to the topic. This is followed by sections focusing on the background to and rationale for your study, as well as the nature and role of play in early year's education. You are to be commended for having read widely. Your section on action research methodology is well-considered and you discuss ethical considerations associated with your study. The following section, on the analysis of research data, is thorough and you set out your main findings concisely. You offer an appropriate concluding section, together with some recommendations for future practice. A question to consider: was it Piaget who said 'Play is the child's work' and 'Play is a serious business?'

Relevance to practice:

Your assignment is successful in demonstrating relationships between educational theory and practice. It is clear that the research undertaken will be beneficial both for your own institution and in terms of your own professional development and practice.

Presentation:

Presentation throughout is of a very high standard. Please see my comments in the text.

References:

I have scanned a selection of references in the text and found all of these in the bibliography. Looking ahead to your dissertation, please consider drawing on a broader range of journal articles to support your arguments. Congratulations on having written an excellent assignment!

Recommended mark: 75
Marking tutor's signature:
Date:

Postgraduate Research Project: Dissertation

Title:

Developing Effective Approaches to the Teaching and Learning of Argument in Religious Education: An Action Research Study.

Introduction/Conclusion:

Your excellent summary and introduction offer a clear and concise rationale for the dissertation. A research project that focuses on developing effective approaches to the teaching and learning of argument in religious education in a secondary school is timely. Based on the research you have undertaken, you offer appropriate conclusions and recommendations for future practice.

Content:

The dissertation focuses on: (1) establishing a rationale for the study through a critical review of relevant literature; (2) outlining the research methods used in your study and examining some key texts in the research methodology literature; (3) discussing ethical considerations associated with the study; (4) setting out and discussing your findings; (5) offering conclusions and recommendations for future practice.

Research Design:

You offer an appropriate rationale for the use of an action research approach and you relate your work to research undertaken previously for the MA degree. You utilise triangulation to good effect, drawing on questionnaires, semi-structured interviews and observations.

Use of Literature:

Your dissertation offers evidence of extensive reading and you are successful throughout in demonstrating relationships between educational theory and practice. It is clear that the research undertaken will have important implications for your school, as well as for your own professional development.

Academic Presentation:

Presentation throughout is of a very high standard. I have scanned a selection of references in the text and found all of these in the bibliography. You have benefited from having produced draft chapters throughout the period of study and you have worked at a consistently high level.

This is an excellent piece of work, which I have enjoyed reading. I hope you will consider publishing some of your dissertation in professional journals. Given the quality of your work, I also suggest that you should consider undertaking a research

⇨

> degree (M.Phil./Ph.D.). If you would like to discuss either publication or beginning a research degree, please let me know. Well done!
>
> *Suggested Mark (First Marker):* 85
>
> *Suggested Mark (Second Marker):*
>
> *Agreed mark (subject to confirmation by the external examiner):*
>
> *Signed:*
>
> *First Marker*
>
> *Signed:*
>
> *Second Marker*

While funded research projects are not assessed in the same way as reports submitted for an academic qualification (i.e. they are not given a mark or grade), it is customary for the funding body to provide some guidance concerning success indicators. For example, this may take the form of advice about how best to approach the individual categories set out in Figure 6.2. For a discussion of how postgraduate research theses are assessed, see Mullins and Kiley (2002).

Comments on action research project assessments

In concluding this chapter, I would like to make some comments about the action research project assessments outlined above. To begin with, it is important that you should consider the issue of assessment *before* undertaking your research project. The best way to do this is to read carefully the information provided in your course or module handbook, which should contain the assessment pro forma(s) being used, as well as general guidance about how to complete your project successfully. If you have any questions about the assessment process, please consult your tutor.

You will see from the first two assessments that there is a substantial variation in students' attainment. Familiarising yourself with the assessment pro forma, asking pertinent questions, and looking at examples of projects completed by previous cohorts of students (please ask your tutor if you can read some of these), will enable you to begin your research in an effective way. This is because you will be able to distinguish between good and less than successful practice from the beginning. Please note that, in their assessment of your work, tutors will draw your attention to those aspects of your project which are to be commended, as well as to those areas that require improvement. Often their feedback will take the form of a commentary on what you have written but tutors may also ask you questions to encourage your reflective thinking and practice. As is evident from the first assessment, such questions may be asked even in the context of excellent research studies. Reflective Thinking Exercise 7.4 focuses on the assessment of your project.

Reflective Thinking Exercise 7.4

1. When your research project has been assessed, consider your tutor's comments and questions.
2. Do you understand these fully?
3. What have you learned?

Do you have any questions for your tutor?

How Do I Publish My Action Research Report? **8**

Chapter Outline

Students' experiences of writing for publication   101

Publishing action research reports in journals   104

Publishing action research reports through presenting
conference papers   105

Having completed your action research report, you may now wish to share your findings with a broader audience. Several authors offer advice on how to do this in the context of: (1) presentations to your colleagues (Baumfield *et al.*, 2008; MacNaughton and Hughes, 2009; Mertler, 2009); (2) the Internet (MacNaughton and Hughes, 2009; Mertler, 2009). Given that two key questions often asked by researchers are: 'Why should I publish my action research report?' and 'How do I publish my action research report?' My aim here is to examine

- students' experiences of writing for publication;
- publishing action research reports in journals;
- publishing action research reports through presenting conference papers.

Students' experiences of writing for publication

There is now a substantial literature on academic writing and publishing (Hartley, 2008; Murray and Moore, 2006), much of which is intended primarily for lecturers and researchers, rather than undergraduate and postgraduate students undertaking taught courses (Aitchison *et al.*, 2010; Wellington, 2003). However, in recent years, the idea of developing undergraduate research has become increasingly popular (Garde-Hansen and Calvert, 2007; Healey and Jenkins, 2009).

In my own university, we have replaced the third year undergraduate dissertation (an assignment of 6000 to 8000 words in length) with a research article (3000 words). As part of a module entitled 'Education and Professional Studies', I offer seminars on topics such as: 'Undertaking a literature review'; 'Action research'; 'Research ethics'; 'Writing a research article' and 'Publishing a research article'. Students are asked to write an article (or paper) for one of three named journals and a visiting professor (who is a former editor of one of the journals) has reviewed some of the best pieces of work and offered additional advice concerning possible publication. Again with a view to developing their reflecting thinking and practice, students have been asked for their views on this assignment (Bassett and Costello, 2009). The following abridged extract from a questionnaire distributed to a cohort of 36 students offers another example of gathering qualitative and quantitative research data (Figure 8.1).

---

1. Do you believe that it is important for teachers to publish their good practice for others to read?

YES **36**   NO **0**   DON'T KNOW **0**

Please give reasons for your view:

- Yes: a great way for others to gain knowledge and teaching ideas; an excellent resource which is more reliable/realistic, as a fellow teacher has written and published this work.
- Yes: because it gives other teachers 'food for thought' on topical issues.
- Yes: it informs good practice and generates further potential to develop one's own pedagogic practice.
- Yes: it enables others to gain a perspective on what constitutes good teaching and how effective it has been.
- Yes: it is always helpful to consider the good practice of others when thinking/reflecting on your own practice.
- Yes: journal articles written by teachers are a good source for other teachers to pick up new techniques.

Figure 8.1 Questionnaire.

2. Did you find writing the research article a challenging assignment?

YES **33**   NO **1**   DON'T KNOW **1**

- Yes: it was very challenging to read broadly and critically analyse what each author has to say.
- Yes: challenging but very worthwhile.
- It is writing in a different style. When choosing your own topic, it made it more challenging as you were in control.
- Yes, it was very challenging and I researched the work thoroughly to write a successful article.
- Yes: I had never written anything like this before; it was the first time that I had critically evaluated current research.

3. Do you believe that you had sufficient choice of area to research?

YES **36**   NO **0**   DON'T KNOW **0**

4. Did you undertake any additional small-scale research to complement your critical review of the literature?

YES **8**   NO **28**

5. Do you feel that this research added to the quality of your research article?

YES **8**   NO **0**   DON'T KNOW **0**

If yes, please give reasons for your view:

- It gave me practical evidence to support the views formed.
- I was able to appreciate what children think when they are engaged in learning through play.
- I was able to see how what I was researching was put into place and how this was being received.

6. If you were doing this assignment again, what three things would you do differently?

- Start earlier/allow more time.
- Read more articles from the journal I am writing for.
- Choose a topic on which there is a lot more published.
- Even more reading is necessary.
- Some small-scale research to give a practical view.
- Be more critical of my first attempts.

Figure 8.1 *Continued.*

Although this form of assessment is relatively new, it has been welcomed by students. In my seminar on publication, I outline ways in which the article (and research projects more generally) may be written up and submitted to a broad range of journals. In the following sections, I shall discuss this, together with making presentations at conferences.

Publishing action research reports in journals

MacNaughton and Hughes (2009, p. 231) argue that the similarities between research project reports and articles for academic journals are such that 'a researcher will often use their formal, written project report as the starting point for a subsequent journal article, rather than starting from scratch'.

If you are considering publishing your action research report in a journal, you should seek advice from your tutor or mentor concerning how to proceed. My own view is that you should begin by considering the range of journals in your particular subject discipline (e.g. Education) or sub-section of it (e.g. primary education) and then find out which of these are available in your HEI's library (either in printed copy or on-line). Then you need to examine the journals carefully and ask yourself the following questions: What subject matter is covered? What guidance do the journals offer about accepting articles for publication?'

Some professional journals ask for shorter articles (fewer than 3000 words). I suggest you begin by aiming to publish in one of these before going on to write lengthier papers (5000–6000 words). You will increase your chance of success by following closely the requirements set out by journals. These relate to matters such as: focusing on appropriate subject content; adhering to the suggested word length; following guidance on quotation and referencing in the text; setting out the bibliography appropriately; and writing a summary of your article if required etc. If the journal you are writing for has a policy of sending papers to referees for their comments, so that they can make a recommendation as to whether your article should be published, pay close attention to their comments and advice. If it is suggested that your article needs to be amended, do not be discouraged; make the changes as suggested and submit your work again. It is much more likely to be accepted when submitted for a second time.

Wellington (2003) interviewed 12 editors of journals in the UK. Here are some of their comments concerning the question 'What counts as a good article?' (pp. 67–68).

- Clear and coherent argument backed up by appropriate data (where relevant); well set out.
- Internal consistency; 'soundness'; is it well written? Does it flow?
- Reads well, lucid, well-organised. Clear evidence of existing knowledge of the topic under investigation; evidence of critical engagement with that and where it will take them; the ability to theorise; to understand the sensitivities of research findings; takes notice of the requirements of the journal.

When asked the questions 'What are grounds for rejection? And common complaints?' the editors responded as follows (pp. 69–70):

- Bad ones: lack any theoretical depth, are not grounded in previous literature, their methodology is inappropriate for the research questions, have short conclusions or discussion, are *just* aimed at classroom practice, but not grounded in any theoretical perspective, show little depth of analysis, 'superficial analysis of data'.
- Really bad?: the author has never opened the pages of this journal. Someone, who has written on a topic, and made no reference to a series of articles on the same topic; I can just look at the list of references to get a feel for this.
- Confused or incoherent writing: no data or evidence, confusing presentation of data.
- Poorly presented, badly written, inadequately argued, lacking a theoretical framework, uninformed by the literature . . . and so on.

For additional guidance on publishing your action research project in a journal and elsewhere, see Murray (2009), Norton (2009), and Wellington (2003).

Publishing action research reports through presenting conference papers

As Norton (2009, p. 200) suggests: 'If you are aiming at a journal paper, presenting your findings at a conference first will give you some valuable peer feedback which will help you develop your paper'. Also, presentations are frequently published in the conference proceedings of the event. In order to have a conference paper accepted, it is customary to submit a proposal (Costello, 2009b). This usually contains several categories and you are asked to write to a specific word limit. Below are examples of proposals I have made to present papers at both a national and an international conference (Figures 8.2 and 8.3).

Once your proposal has been accepted, you will need to consider how to present your paper (Karlin, 2008). Conference speakers usually prepare a PowerPoint presentation and the easiest way to do this is to follow the main points outlined in your proposal (Figure 8.4).

Title of Paper
Developing Communities of Inquiry in the UK: Retrospect and Prospect

Abstract
(maximum 250 words)

My aim in this paper is to offer a critical evaluation of the development of communities of inquiry (CoI) in the UK, with particular reference to the teaching of philosophical thinking in schools. The paper is divided into four sections. In the first, I offer an answer to the question 'what is a community of inquiry?' and examine some key aspects of the development of CoI from an historical perspective. The second section focuses on the question: 'should children be taught to think philosophically?' Following this and drawing on my own research, I outline my approach to the teaching of philosophy to young children and discuss the current context for such teaching in the UK. Finally, I conclude by considering future prospects for developing CoI. I shall argue that such development is likely to take place within the context of the following themes:

- The increasing prominence of (and importance attributed to) teachers' research projects.
- The growth of organisations that aim to promote the teaching and learning of thinking skills (including Philosophy).
- The prevalence of publications in this field.
- New directions for research and practice.

In the context of the conference theme, I shall argue that the teaching of philosophical thinking in schools offers an excellent example of 'education beyond boundaries', since it enables learners to reflect critically on a broad range of subject matter. Such reflection may be exercised in the context of (but will not be limited to) the formal school curriculum.

247 words

Figure 8.2 Proposal to present a paper at a national conference.

Title of Presentation: Tolerance, Citizenship Education and the Development of Moral Values

Abstract (maximum 100 words)

My central aim in this paper is to explore the role of the school in the development of tolerance and other moral values. I argue that effective citizenship education programmes, that incorporate the teaching of philosophical thinking skills in schools, have an important contribution to make to this endeavour. Having examined the relationship between citizenship education and the teaching of philosophy in schools, I outline my own approach to the latter and suggest that the teaching of critical thinking, reasoning and argument skills is essential to the development of tolerance and other moral values. [94 words]

Summary (maximum 500 words)

My central aim in this paper is to explore the role of the school in the development of tolerance and other moral values. I shall argue that effective citizenship education programmes, that incorporate the teaching of philosophical thinking skills, have a substantial contribution to make to this endeavour. I begin by responding to the question 'why educate for tolerance?' This is followed by the presentation of arguments for developing tolerance and other moral values within the context of citizenship education programmes. Having discussed the nature of citizenship education and argued for the concept of a 'reflective citizenry', I explore the relationship between such education and the teaching of philosophy in schools.

The idea that children should engage in the systematic discussion of philosophical ideas is a relatively new one. My aim here is to offer a rationale for such an endeavour. In the USA, there has emerged what has been called 'a new branch of philosophy', Philosophy for Children. The main pioneer of this field of philosophy is Matthew Lipman and, in this part of the paper, I offer a critical examination of his 'Philosophy for Children' programme. Drawing on my own research (e.g. *Thinking Skills and Early Childhood Education*, David Fulton Publishers), I outline my own approach to the teaching of philosophy to young children and examine findings of research studies concerned with improving the quality of children's thinking, reasoning and argument skills.

In the context of the conference theme, I argue that teaching such skills in schools is essential to the development of tolerance and other moral values. The main points of the presentation are: Why educate for tolerance?; Tolerance, moral values and citizenship education; What is citizenship education?; Citizenship education and the teaching of philosophy in schools; The nature of philosophical thinking; Teaching philosophical thinking skills: the 'Philosophy for Children' programme; Developing moral values through the teaching of philosophical thinking in British schools; Improving the quality of children's argument; Assessing progress in argument; Cultivating tolerance: the role of the school. [333 words]

Key words
Tolerance
Citizenship education
Moral values
Philosophy in schools

Figure 8.3 Proposal to present a paper at an international conference.

Thirty-Fifth Conference of the Association for Moral Education

'Cultivating Tolerance: Moral Functioning and its Development'

Utrecht University, The Netherlands

Tolerance, Citizenship Education and the Development of Moral Values

Professor Patrick Costello

Glyndŵr University, Wales

Why educate for tolerance?

- Tolerance, moral values and citizenship education
- 'A key component of civic education is to teach children the virtues of liberal, democratic citizenship . . . toleration, mutual respect, reciprocity . . .' (MacMullen)
- The nature of citizenship education

Figure 8.4 PowerPoint presentation

The nature of philosophical thinking

- Education for citizenship and the concept of a reflective citizenry
- Citizenship and the teaching of philosophy
- What is philosophy?
- Why teach philosophical thinking in schools?
- Philosophy and the development of moral values

Developing philosophical thinking skills

- The 'Philosophy for Children' programme
- Lipman's 'community of inquiry'
- Developing philosophical thinking in British schools
- Developing moral values: teaching philosophy through narrative and video

The teaching and learning of argument

- Improving the quality of young children's argument
- Assessing progress in argument

Figure 8.4 *Continued.*

Cultivating tolerance: the role of the school

- General learning goals: values, knowledge and skills
- Tolerance and the teaching of thinking, reasoning and argument skills
- Schools as communities of inquiry: an alternative vision of education?

References

- Blommaert, J. (1998) *Debating Diversity: Analysing the Rhetoric of Tolerance*, London: Routledge.
- Brunskill, K. (2006) *Developing Consideration, Respect and Tolerance*, London: Paul Chapman.
- Costello, P.J.M. (2000) *Thinking Skills and Early Childhood Education*, London: David Fulton Publishers.
- Costello, P.J.M. (2003) *Action Research*, London: Continuum.
- Costello, P.J.M. (2010) 'Developing communities of inquiry in the UK: retrospect and prospect', *Analytic Teaching: The Community of Inquiry Journal* (forthcoming).
- MacMullen, I. (2007) *Faith in Schools? Autonomy, Citizenship and Religious Education in the Liberal State*, Oxford: Princeton University Press.
- UNESCO (1994) *Tolerance: The Threshold of Peace*, Paris: UNESCO.
- Vogt, W. Paul (1997) *Tolerance and Education: Learning to Live with Diversity and Difference*, London: Sage.

Figure 8.4 *Continued.*

Reflective Thinking Exercise 8.1 focuses on publishing your action research project report in a journal.

Reflective Thinking Exercise 8.1

1. Find a journal that relates to your action research project.
2. Look at the content and structure of several articles.
3. Write a draft article using the structure of one of these published papers.
4. Discuss the article with your tutor or mentor.

Recommended Further Reading   9

Chapter Outline

The importance of reading widely   113
Recommended further reading   114

The importance of reading widely

As I stated at the beginning of this book, its central aims are to enable practitioners to undertake and to offer an account of an action research project. When developing such a project (for example, as part of a course of study for an academic qualification), I suggested that it is important to read widely. This will enable you both to increase your knowledge and understanding of educational theory and practice, and to underpin your research with relevant references to the literature.

While this volume provides a concise introduction to action research, a number of other texts offer important insights into (and sometimes extensive accounts of) its key features. With this in mind, you may find helpful the following suggestions for further reading. Please remember that these are *examples* from what is now a substantial body of written work in this area. It is part of the task of undertaking research that you should reflect critically on source material beyond that suggested by your tutor. The texts indicated below will, in turn, offer their own suggestions for further reading.

Recommended further reading

It is advisable to read some accounts of action research that are located within general texts concerned with undertaking educational or social science research, such as Bassey (1998), Bell (2005), Blaxter *et al.* (2001), Denscombe (2007), Hopkins (2008) and Robson (2002). Having considered how action research relates to other forms or types of research, you can then move on to books with a specific action research focus, such as Baumfield *et al.* (2008), Coghlan and Brannick (2005), Macintyre (2000), McNiff and Whitehead (2006), Mertler (2009), Norton (2009) and Somekh (2006).

For discussions about

- *the origins of action research*, see Adelman (1993), Coghlan and Brannick, (2005), Elliott (1991), Hopkins (2008), McNiff and Whitehead (2006) and Norton (2009);
- *models of action research*, see Baumfield *et al.* (2008), Coghlan and Brannick (2005), Drummond and Themessl-Huber (2007), Elliott (1991), Hopkins (2008), MacNaughton and Hughes (2009), McNiff with Whitehead (2002) and Mertler (2009).
- *ethical considerations in undertaking action research*, see Blaxter *et al.* (2001), British Educational Research Association (2004), Denscombe (2009), Gregory (2003); Hostetler (2005); Norton (2009), Oliver (2010) and Thomas (2009).
- *criteria for good action research*, see Coghlan and Brannick (2005), Elliott (1995), Feldman (2007), MacNaughton and Hughes (2009) and Mertler (2009).

Much useful information about action research may be found via the Internet. In particular, Southern Cross University (2009) in Australia offers a substantial archive of resource material. Of particular interest to beginning researchers is the collection of papers supporting a 14-week introductory course, 'Action Research and Evaluation on Line', and a series of brief comments about action research, 'Occasional Pieces'. If you are proposing to undertake a postgraduate action research project, I suggest you read Dick's (1993) 'You want to do an action research thesis?', which offers guidance on key issues and contains a substantial (and annotated) bibliography. In addition, Mertler (2009, pp. 206–7) provides details of a number of action research electronic journals.

Within the UK, the Collaborative Action Research Network (CARN), whose website is hosted by Manchester Metropolitan University, 'aims to encourage and support action research projects (personal, local, national and international), accessible accounts of action research projects, and contributions to the theory and methodology of action research' (see CARN, 2010). The website contains information about becoming a member of the Network, as well as details of its study days, conferences and publications (including CARN Bulletins and the journal *Educational Action Research*). Links to related websites are also provided.

The 'Teachers' TV' website has a section which focuses on case studies investigating the use of action research in schools (see http://www.teachers.tv/video/4883).

A number of books and other sources offer very useful advice and guidance on: undertaking a literature search and review, research ethics, and collecting and analysing action research data. In particular, see the following for information concerning

- *literature search and review*: Birmingham City University (2007), Cridland (2008), Hart (1998, 2001), MacNaughton and Hughes (2009), Mertler (2009), Rumsey (2008) and Thomas (2009);
- *quantitative and qualitative research*: Blaxter *et al.* (2001), Denscombe (2007), Freebody (2003), Maxwell (2005), Robson (2002), Thomas (2009) and Wragg (1999);
- *case study research*: Bassey (1999), Gillham (2000), Simons (2009) and Yin (2009);
- *questionnaires*: Bell (2005), Denscombe (2007), Gillham (2008a, 2008c), Macintyre (2000), and Robson (2002);
- *interviews*: Bell (2005), Denscombe (2007), Gillham (2001, 2005, 2008c), James and Busher (2009), Macintyre (2000) and Robson (2002);
- *observation studies*: Bell (2005), Denscombe (2007), Gillham (2008b), Macintyre (2000), Robson (2002) and Wragg (1999);
- *audiotape recording/videotape recording*: Baumfield *et al.* (2008), Hopkins (2008), Macintyre (2000), Mertler (2009) and Wragg (1999);
- *diaries, journals and field notes*: Baumfield *et al.* (2008), Bell (2005), Hopkins (2008), Macintyre (2000), Mertler (2009), Moon (2006), Patrick *et al.* (2007) and Thomas (2009).

Endnote: The Theory and Practice of Action Research **10**

Chapter Outline

Rationale for the format of this book   117
Developing reflective thinking and practice   118

Rationale for the format of this book

In conclusion, I would like to offer a rationale for the format I have chosen to adopt in writing this book. Although it is customary to outline this at the beginning of a volume, I have chosen a different approach here. This is for two reasons. First, as I said in the introduction, my main aims have been to enable you to undertake effective action research and to offer an account of an action research project. Given this (and the overall length of the book), my primary emphasis has been on the *practice* of action research, underpinned as necessary by references to educational theory. To offer a substantial rationale at the beginning may have detracted from the essentially practical focus of the text.

The second reason for selecting this approach is that I wanted you to experience each part of the action research process without having to undertake too much preliminary thinking about its individual stages. I find that this strategy is particularly useful, both for practitioners who are embarking on their first research project and for those who may not have undertaken such work for a number of years. This is because it should help to dispel potential anxieties that would-be researchers may have concerning the nature of the project, the methodologies involved, the theoretical reflection required, etc. Having examined these key issues individually and given some thought to how they might be addressed in the context of your own educational practice, you should now be ready to embark on your project.

Developing reflective thinking and practice

To assist you in this, the format of the book is intended to offer guidance at each stage of the process. Throughout, my focus has been on the development of reflective thinking and practice. With this in mind and in thinking about how to begin, I suggest you look again at the eight key action research questions and then consider the following: What do you understand is meant by 'action research'? What are the similarities and differences between different models of action research? Is there a particular model of action research that appeals to you because it would be useful in helping you to structure your project? Could you develop your own model of action research from existing models?

Now ask yourself the question 'Why should I undertake action research?' and examine the issues discussed in Chapter 2. Which of these issues is relevant to your own professional practice? Do you regard yourself as a 'reflective practitioner' and, if so, why? Should teachers engage in research and should teaching move increasingly towards being a research-based profession? Having considered the problems with educational research that were outlined, how might these be overcome? Finally, what do you consider to be the role of research in bringing about school improvement and in enhancing your own professional development?

As regards your action research project, you need to consider the following questions in the early stages of your work: Have you attended those research methodology seminars that may have been provided to support your study? Have you undertaken a thorough literature search and review? Do you have questions to ask before you develop your research proposal? Who might be able to answer these? Having produced the research proposal, have you made any amendments that may have been suggested by your tutor or mentor? Have you examined available research reports produced by other researchers? Do you understand how your action research report will be assessed? If not, who might be able to advise you on this?

When you have completed a literature search and gained access to a broad range of source material, you will need to evaluate critically what authors have said about those educational (and other) issues with which you are concerned. In order to do this, you may utilise both quotation and citation in the text. Throughout this book, I have quoted from and cited a number of sources. In doing so, my intention has been

1. to illustrate relationships between educational theory and practice;
2. to offer practical examples of quotation and citation, so that you can consider how these might be incorporated into your project.

Before attempting to collect and analyse research data, examine again the criticisms of action research that I discussed in Chapter 4. Having done this, consider the following key question: 'How can I ensure that my research is as rigorous as possible?'

Before producing your research report, look carefully again at both the guidance offered by your own HEI or funding body, and that outlined in Chapter 6. When your research report has been assessed, reflect on the feedback you have received from your marking tutor and ask yourself what you have learned regarding

1. the project itself;
2. other assignments that you may still have to complete.

If you have produced a very good piece of work and are interested in exploring the possibility that some (or all) of it might be published, discuss this with your tutor. Finally, please remember that, in order to increase your understanding of the central themes of this book, it is important to read widely. To this end, I have made a number of suggestions for further reading in Chapter 9. I wish you success in your research!

Bibliography

Adelman, C. (1993) 'Kurt Lewin and the origins of action research', *Educational Action Research*, Vol. 1, No. 1, pp. 7–24.

Aitchison, C., Kamler, B. and Lee, A. (2010) *Publishing Pedagogies for the Doctorate and Beyond*, Abingdon: Routledge.

Bassett, P. and Costello, P. J. M. (2009) 'Towards teachers as practitioner researchers: encouraging undergraduate trainees to publish'. Paper presented at the Fifth Annual ESCalate Initial Teacher Education Conference, Glyndŵr University Wrexham, 15 May.

Bassey, M. (1998) 'Action research for improving educational practice', in Halsall, R. (ed.) *Teacher Research and School Improvement: Opening Doors from the Inside*, Buckingham: Open University Press, pp. 93–108.

Bassey, M. (1999) *Case Study Research in Educational Settings*, Buckingham: Open University Press.

Baumfield, V., Hall, E. and Wall, K. (2008) *Action Research in the Classroom*, London: Sage.

Bell, J. (1987) *Doing Your Research Project: A Guide for First-Time Researchers in Education and Social Science*, Buckingham: Open University Press.

Bell, J. (2005) *Doing Your Research Project: A Guide for First-Time Researchers in Education and Social Science*, 4th edn, Buckingham: Open University Press.

Birmingham City University (2007) 'How to write a literature review', http://www.ssdd.bcu.ac.uk/learner/writingguides/1.04.htm

Blaxter, L., Hughes, C. and Tight, M. (2001) *How to Research*, 2nd edn, Buckingham: Open University Press.

Bolton, G. (2005) *Reflective Practice: Writing and Professional Development*, 2nd edn, London: Sage.

British Educational Research Association (2004) *Revised Ethical Guidelines for Educational Research*, http://www.bera.ac.uk/publications/guidelines.

Burgess, H., Sieminski, S. and Arthur, L. (2006) *Achieving Your Doctorate in Education*, London: Sage.

Burke, V., Jones, I. and Doherty, M. (2005) 'Analysing student perceptions of transferable skills via undergraduate degree programmes', *Active Learning in Higher Education*, Vol. 6, No. 2, pp. 132–44.

Burkhardt, H. and Schoenfeld, A. H. (2003) 'Improving educational research: toward a more useful, more influential, and better-funded enterprise', *Educational Researcher*, Vol. 32, No. 9, pp. 3–14.

Campbell, A. (2007) 'Practitioner research', London: TLRP, http://www.bera.ac.uk/practitioner-research/.

CARN (2010) 'Collaborative Action Research Network', http://www.did.stu.mmu.ac.uk/carnnew.

Carter, K. and Halsall, R. (1998) 'Teacher research for school improvement', in Halsall, R. (ed.) *Teacher Research and School Improvement: Opening Doors from the Inside*, Buckingham: Open University Press, pp.71–90.

Coghlan, D. and Brannick, T. (2005) *Doing Action Research in Your Own Organisation*, 2nd edn, London: Sage.

Coleman, A. (2007) 'Leaders as researchers: supporting practitioner enquiry through the NCSL research associate programme', *Educational Management Administration and Leadership*, Vol. 35, No. 4, pp. 479–97.

Costello, P. J. M. (2000) *Thinking Skills and Early Childhood Education*, London: David Fulton Publishers.

Costello, P. J. M. (2003) *Action Research*, London: Continuum.

Costello, P. J. M. (2007a) 'Developing teachers' research into the teaching of thinking skills in Wales', *Prospero: A Journal of New Thinking in Philosophy for Education*, Vol. 13, No. 1, pp. 38–44.

Costello, P. J. M. (2007b) 'Writing reflectively and effectively: developing the skills of critical thinking, reasoning and argument in higher education', *Reflections on Higher Education*, Vol. 15, pp. 58–71.

Costello, P. J. M. (2009a) 'Can we teach students in higher education to think critically?', *Education Today*, Vol. 59, No. 1, pp. 20–5.

Costello, P. J. M. (2009b) 'Tolerance, citizenship education and the development of moral values'. Paper presented at the Thirty-Fifth Conference of the Association for Moral Education, 'Cultivating Tolerance: Moral Functioning and its Development', Utrecht University, The Netherlands, 3 July.

Cridland, C. (2008) 'Writing the literature review', Monash University, Australia, http://www.sci.monash.edu.au/postgrad/docs/seminars/0508pglitreview.ppt

Cryer, P. (2006) *The Research Student's Guide to Success*, 3rd edn, Buckingham: Open University Press.

Denscombe, M. (2007) *The Good Research Guide for Small-Scale Social Research Projects*, 3rd edn, Buckingham: Open University Press.

Denscombe, M. (2009) *Ground Rules for Social Research: Guidelines for Good Practice*, 2nd edn, Buckingham: Open University Press.

Dick, B. (1993) 'You want to do an action research thesis?', http://www.scu.edu.au/schools/gcm/ar/art/arthesis.html

Dick, B. (1997) 'Action learning and action research', http://www.scu.edu.au/schools/gcm/ar/arp/actlearn.html

Dick, B. (2000) 'Postgraduate programmes using action research', http://www.scu.edu.au/schools/gcm/ar/arp/ppar.html

Dick, B. (2002) 'Action research: action *and* research', http://www.scu.edu.au/schools/gcm/ar/arp/aandr.html

Dick, B. (2004) 'Action research literature: themes and trends', *Action Research*, Vol. 2, No. 4, pp. 425–44.

Dick, B. (2006) 'Action research literature 2004–2006: themes and trends', *Action Research*, Vol. 4, No. 4, pp. 439–58.

Dick, B. (2009) 'Action research literature 2006–2008: themes and trends', *Action Research*, Vol. 7, No. 4, pp. 423–41.

Drummond, J. S. and Themessl-Huber, M. (2007) 'The cyclical process of action research', *Action Research*, Vol. 5, No.4, pp. 430–48.

Durkin, K. and Main, A. (2002) 'Discipline-based study skills support for first-year undergraduate students', *Active Learning in Higher Education*, Vol. 3, No. 1, pp. 24–39.

Egan, D. and James, R. (2002) *An Evaluation for the General Teaching Council for Wales of the Professional Development Pilot Projects 2001–2002*, Bristol: PPI Group.

Egan, D. and James, R. (2003) *Final Report of the Evaluation of the General Teaching Council for Wales Phase 2 Professional Development Pilot Projects 2002–2003*, Bristol: PPI Group.

Egan, D. and James, R. (2004) *Evaluation for the General Teaching Council for Wales of the Phase 3 Professional Development Pilot Projects: Final Report*, Bristol: PPI Group.

Elliott, J. (1991) *Action Research for Educational Change*, Buckingham: Open University Press.

Elliott, J. (1995) 'What is good action research? – some criteria', *Action Researcher*, No. 2, pp. 10–1.

Feldman, A. (2007) 'Validity and quality in action research', *Educational Action Research*, Vol. 15, No. 1, pp. 21–32.

Foskett, N., Lumby, J. and Fidler, B. (2005) 'Evolution or extinction? Reflections on the future of research in educational leadership and management', *Educational Management Administration and Leadership*, Vol. 33, No. 2, pp. 245–53.

Freebody, P. (2003) *Qualitative Research in Education: Interaction and Practice*, London: Sage.

Frost, P. (2002) 'Principles of the action research cycle', in Ritchie, R., Pollard, A., Frost, P. and Eaude, T. (eds) *Action Research: A Guide for Teachers. Burning Issues in Primary Education*, Issue No. 3, Birmingham: National Primary Trust, pp. 24–32.

Furlong, J. and Salisbury, J. (2005) 'Best Practice Research Scholarships: an evaluation', *Research Papers in Education*, Vol. 20, No. 1, pp. 45–83.

Garde-Hansen, J. and Calvert, B. (2007) 'Developing a research culture in the undergraduate curriculum', *Active Learning in Higher Education*, Vol. 8, No. 2, pp. 105–16.

General Teaching Council for Wales (2002a) *Continuing Professional Development: An Entitlement for All*, Cardiff: GTCW.

General Teaching Council for Wales (2002b) *Professional Development Pilot Projects: Information Booklet 2002–2003*, Cardiff: GTCW.

Gibbs, G. and Dunbat-Goddet, H. (2007) *The Effects of Programme Assessment Environments on Student Learning*, York: The Higher Education Academy.

Gillham, B. (2000) *Case Study Research Methods*, London: Continuum.

Gillham, B. (2001) *The Research Interview*, London: Continuum.

Gillham, B. (2005) *Research Interviewing: The Range of Techniques*, Maidenhead: Open University Press.

Gillham, B. (2008a) *Developing a Questionnaire*, 2nd edn, London: Continuum.

Gillham, B. (2008b) *Observation Techniques: Structured to Unstructured*, London: Continuum.

Gillham, B. (2008c) *Small-Scale Social Survey Methods*, London: Continuum.

Goldfinch, J. and Hughes, M. (2007) 'Skills, learning styles and success of first-year undergraduates', *Active Learning in Higher Education*, Vol. 8, No. 3, pp. 259–73.

Gorard, S. (2004) 'The British Educational Research Association and the future of educational research', *Educational Studies*, Vol. 30, No. 1, pp. 65–76.

Gorard, S. (2005) 'Current contexts for research in educational leadership and management', *Educational Management Administration and Leadership*, Vol. 33, No. 2, pp. 155–64.

Gregory, I. (2003) *Ethics in Research*, London: Continuum.

Halsall, R. (ed.) (1998) *Teacher Research and School Improvement: Opening Doors from the Inside*, Buckingham: Open University Press.

Hargreaves, D. (1996) 'Teaching as a research-based profession: possibilities and prospects', Teacher Training Agency Annual Lecture, April.

Hargreaves, D. (1999) 'Revitalising educational research: lessons from the past and proposals for the future', *Cambridge Journal of Education*, Vol. 29, No. 2, pp. 239–49.

Hart, C. (1998) *Doing a Literature Review: Releasing the Social Science Research Imagination*, London: Sage.

Hart, C. (2001) *Doing a Literature Search: A Comprehensive Guide for the Social Sciences*, London: Sage.

Hartley, J. (2008) *Academic Writing and Publishing: A Practical Handbook*, Oxford: Routledge.

Healey, M. and Jenkins, A. (2009) *Developing Undergraduate Research and Inquiry*, York: The Higher Education Academy.

Hedberg, P. R. (2009) 'Learning through reflective classroom practice', *Journal of Management Education*, Vol. 33, No. 1, pp. 10–36.

Hillage, J., Pearson, R., Anderson, A. and Tamkin, P. (1998) *Excellence in Research on Schools*, Research Report No. 74, Norwich: Her Majesty's Stationery Office.

Hopkins, D. (2008) *A Teacher's Guide to Classroom Research*, 4th edn, Buckingham: Open University Press.

Hostetler, K. (2005) 'What is "good" education research?', *Educational Researcher*, Vol. 34, No. 6, pp. 16–21.

James, N. and Busher, H. (2009) *Online Interviewing*, London: Sage.

Judge, B., Jones, P. and McCreery, E. (2009) *Critical Thinking Skills for Education Students*, Exeter: Learning Matters.

Karlin, N. J. (2008) 'Creating an effective conference presentation', http://www.kon.org/karlin.html

Kuit, J. A., Reay, G. and Freeman, R. (2001) 'Experiences of reflective teaching', *Active Learning in Higher Education*, Vol. 2, No. 2, pp. 128–42.

Lewin, K. (1946) 'Action research and minority problems', *Journal of Social Issues*, Vol. 2, No. 4, pp. 34–46.

Loughran, J. J. (2002) 'Effective reflective practice: in search of meaning in learning about teaching', *Journal of Teacher Education*, Vol. 53, No. 1, pp. 33–43.

McGill, I. and Beaty, L. (2001) *Action Learning: A Guide for Professional, Management and Educational Development*, 2nd edn, London: Kogan Page.

Macintyre, C. (2000) *The Art of Action Research in the Classroom*, London: David Fulton Publishers.

MacNaughton, G. and Hughes, P. (2009) *Doing Action Research in Early Childhood Studies: A Step by Step Guide*, Maidenhead: Open University Press.

McNiff, J. with Whitehead, J. (2002) *Action Research: Principles and Practice*, 2nd edn, London: RoutledgeFalmer.

McNiff, J. and Whitehead, J. (2006) *All You Need to Know about Action Research*, London: Sage.

Matthiesen, J. and Binder, M. (2009) *How to Survive Your Doctorate*, Maidenhead: Open University Press.

Maxwell, J. A. (1992) 'Understanding and validity in qualitative research', *Harvard Educational Review*, Vol. 62, No. 3, pp. 279–300.

Maxwell, J. A. (2005) *Qualitative Research Design: An Interactive Approach*, 2nd edn, London: Sage.

Mertler, C. A. (2009) *Action Research: Teachers as Researchers in the Classroom*, 2nd edn, London: Sage.

Moon, J. (2005) *We Seek it Here . . . A New Perspective on the Elusive Activity of Critical Thinking: A Theoretical and Practical Approach*, Bristol: The Higher Education Academy/ESCalate.

Moon, J. (2006) *Learning Journals: A Handbook for Reflective Practice and Professional Development*, 2nd edn, London: Routledge.

Moseley, D., Elliott, J., Gregson, M. and Higgins, S. (2005) 'Thinking skills frameworks for use in education and training', *British Educational Research Journal*, Vol. 31, No.3, pp. 367–90.

Mullins, G. and Kiley, M. (2002) 'It's a PhD, not a Nobel Prize: how experienced examiners assess research theses', *Studies in Higher Education*, Vol. 27, No. 4, pp. 369–86.

Murray, R. (2009) *Writing for Academic Journals*, 2nd edn, Maidenhead: Open University Press.

Murray, R. and Moore, S. (2006) *The Handbook of Academic Writing: A Fresh Approach*, Maidenhead: Open University Press.

Mutch, A. (2003) 'Exploring the practice of feedback to students', *Active Learning in Higher Education*, Vol. 4, No. 1, pp. 24–38.

Neville, C. (2010) *The Complete Guide to Referencing and Avoiding Plagiarism*, 2nd edn, Maidenhead: Open University Press.

Norton, L. S. (2009) *Action Research in Teaching and Learning: A Practical Guide to Conducting Pedagogical Research in Universities*, Abingdon: Routledge.

O'Hear, A. (1988) *Who Teaches the Teachers?* London: The Social Affairs Unit.

O'Hear, A. (1989) 'Teachers can become qualified in practice', *The Guardian*, 24 January, p. 23.

Oliver, P. (2010) *The Student's Guide to Research Ethics*, 2nd edn, Maidenhead: Open University Press.

Oxford Learning Institute (undated) 'Giving and receiving feedback', http://www.learning.ox.ac.uk/rsv.php?page=319

Patrick, K. F., McCormack, A. and Reynolds, R. (2007) 'Academic partners mentoring action research: reflecting on the learning process from multiple perspectives', in Townsend, A. (ed.) *Differing Perceptions of the Participative Elements of Action Research*, CARN Bulletin 12, pp. 3–19.

Phillips, E. M. and Pugh, D. S. (2005) *How to Get a Ph.D.: A Handbook for Students and Their Supervisors*, 4th edn, Buckingham: Open University Press.

Pitts, S. E. (2005) 'Testing, testing . . . how do students use written feedback?', *Active Learning in Higher Education*, Vol. 6, No. 3, pp. 218–29.

Pollard, A. (ed.) (2002) *Readings for Reflective Teaching*, London: Continuum.

Pollard, A. with Anderson, J., Maddock, M., Swaffield, S., Warin, J. and Warwick, P. (2008) *Reflective Teaching: Evidence-informed Professional Practice*, 3rd edn, London: Continuum.

Prestage, S., Perks, P. and Soares, A. (2002) 'The DfES model for Best Practice Research Scholarships: tensions', *Management in Education*, Vol. 16, No. 2, pp. 14–17.

Radford, M. (2006) 'Researching classrooms: complexity and chaos', *British Educational Research Journal*, Vol. 32, No. 2, pp. 177–90.

Rae, A. M. and Cochrane, D. K. (2008) 'Listening to students: how to make written assessment feedback useful', *Active Learning in Higher Education*, Vol. 9, No. 3, pp. 217–30.

Riehl, C. (2006) 'Feeling better: a comparison of medical research and education research', *Educational Researcher*, Vol. 35, No. 5, pp. 24–9.

Ritchie, R., Pollard, A., Frost, P. and Eaude, T. (eds) (2002) *Action Research: A Guide for Teachers. Burning Issues in Primary Education*, Issue No. 3, Birmingham: National Primary Trust.

Robson, C. (2002) *Real World Research*, 2nd edn, Oxford: Wiley-Blackwell.

Rose, R. (2002) 'Teaching as a "research-based profession": encouraging practitioner research in special education', *British Journal of Special Education*, Vol. 29, No. 1, pp. 44–8.

Rumsey, S. (2008) *How to Find Information: A Guide for Researchers*, Maidenhead: Open University Press.

Schön, D. A. (1991a) *Educating the Reflective Practitioner*, San Francisco: Jossey-Bass Publishers.

Schön, D. A. (1991b) *The Reflective Practitioner: How Professionals Think in Action*, Aldershot: Avebury.

Schön, D. A. (1992) *The Reflective Turn: Case Studies in and on Educational Practice*, New York: Teachers College Press.

Simons, H. (2009) *Case Study Research in Practice*, London: Sage.

Slavin, R. E. (2002) 'Evidence-based education policies: transforming educational practice and research', *Educational Researcher*, Vol. 31, No. 7, pp. 15–21.

Somekh, B. (2006) *Action Research: A Methodology for Change and Development*, Maidenhead: Open University Press.

Southern Cross University (2009) 'Action research resources', http://www.scu.edu.au/schools/gcm/ar/arhome.html.

Stenhouse, L. (1975) *An Introduction to Curriculum Research and Development*, London: Heinemann.

Stenhouse, L. (1981) 'What counts as research?', *British Journal of Educational Studies*, Vol. 29, No. 2, pp. 103–14.

Taggart, G. L. and Wilson, A. P. (2005) *Promoting Reflective Thinking in Teachers: 50 Action Strategies*, 2nd edn, Thousand Oaks, CA: Corwin Press.

Teachers.tv (undated) 'Action research', http://www.teachers.tv/video/4883.

Thomas, G. (2009) *How to do Your Research Project*, London: Sage.

Tooley, J. with Darby, D. (1998) *Educational Research: A Critique*, London: Office for Standards in Education.

Trafford, V. and Leshem, S. (2008) *Stepping Stones to Achieving Your Doctorate: Focusing on Your Viva from the Start*, Maidenhead: Open University Press.

Wellington, J. (2003) *Getting Published: A Guide for Lecturers and Researchers*, London: RoutledgeFalmer.

Wellington, J., Bathmaker, A-M., Hunt, C., McCulloch, G. and Sikes, P. (2005) *Succeeding with Your Doctorate*, London: Sage.

Wragg, E. C. (1999) *An Introduction to Classroom Observation*, 2nd edn, London: Routledge.

Yin, R. K. (2009) *Case Study Research: Design and Methods*, 4th edn, London: Sage.

York-Barr, J., Sommers, W. A., Ghere, G. S. and Montie, J. (2006) *Reflective Practice to Improve Schools: An Action Guide for Educators*, 2nd edn, Thousand Oaks, CA: Corwin Press.

Index

action research
  arguments/rationales for undertaking 1,
    13, 15
  as apprenticeship 19
  assessing report 1, 87, 98–9
    assessing progress in argument 88–90
    examples of 93–8
    students' views of assessment 91–3
  benefits to teachers from
    undertaking 25
  choosing research topic 31–2
  competencies and skills required for 19
  criticisms of 12–13, 39, 52–7, 119
  cycle 8–9, 11–12, 74
  developing research proposal 32–3, 113
  developing/undertaking project 1, 8, 18,
    38–9, 42–3
  defining characteristics 7
  definitions 5–7
  effective 1–2, 117
  ethical issues 46–51, 114
  examining completed reports 40, 42, 118
  generalisability of findings from 54–6
  guidelines for completing project 38
  importance of 28
  intuitive-proactive 52
  invented examples of 10–11, 13, 45, 57–63
  nature of 1, 5–8
  nature of project 40, 117–18
  models of 8–13, 57, 73–4, 114, 118
  origins of 8, 114
  producing/writing report 1, 119
    acknowledgements 81–2
    appendices 83

bibliography 83
chapters 82–4
citation and referencing 38, 85, 119
conclusions 84
contents page 81
continuity and progression 84
declaration 81
example of structure 79–84
introduction 82–3
plagiarism 85
proofreading 86
quotation 85, 119
recommendations 84
requirements and guidelines
  for 79–86
summary 81
writing style 84–5
publishing report 1, 101, 119
  in journals 104–5
  students' experiences of writing for
    publication 101–4
  through presenting conference
    papers 105–10
rational-reactive 52
rigour in 39, 52–7, 86, 119
small-scale studies 54, 56
structuring project 13
theory and practice of 117–19
thesis 10, 114
undertaken for academic award 19, 45,
  79, 113
utilising to achieve educational
  goals 52
value of 39

Adelman, C. 20, 114
Aitchison, C. 102
argument 2
  model of 63, 76, 88–90
audit trail 55–6

Bassett, P. 102
Bassey, M. 5, 10, 32, 114–15
Baumfield, V. 101, 114–15
Beaty, L. 61
Bell, J. 5, 54, 59, 72, 114–15
Best Practice Research Scholarship
    programme 24
Binder, M. 10
Birmingham City University 35, 115
Blaxter, L. 4, 52–3, 114–15
Bolton, G. 2, 16
Brannick, T. 5, 8, 114
British Educational Research Association
    (BERA) 114
Burgess, H. 5, 10
Burke, V. 2
Burkhardt, H. 22
Busher, H. 115

Calvert, B. 102
Campbell, A. 21
Carter, K. 23
Cochrane, D.K. 87
Coghlan, D. 5, 8, 114
Coleman, A. 6, 21, 24
Collaborative Action Research Network
    (CARN) 114–15
continuing professional development of
    teachers 24–8, 52, 118
Costello, P.J.M. 1–2, 24, 62–3, 77, 88, 91,
    102, 106
Cridland, C. 34–5, 115
critical
  enquiry 5, 19
  engagement 8
  evaluation 119
  reasoning 13
  reflection 9, 11, 74, 113
  thinking 1–2

Cryer, P. 10
Current Education and Children's Services
    Research (CERUK) 34

Darby, D. 21
Denscombe, M. 7, 11, 13, 46, 53, 57, 73–4,
    114–15
Department for Children, Schools and
    Families (DCSF) 59
Dick, B. 1, 5, 7, 9, 10, 12, 18–19, 53, 56, 114
Drummond, J.S. 8, 114
Dunbat-Goddet, H. 87
Durkin, K. 2

Eaude, T. 98
Education-line 34
educational practice 17–20, 28, 34, 45, 113
  improving 22
educational research,
  critical scrutiny of 21
  general texts on 114
  nature of 3, 5, 21
  problems with 21–3, 52, 77, 118
educational settings 3, 9, 13
educational theory 17–20, 28, 34, 45,
    113, 117
  testing 21
Egan, D. 25
Elliott, J. 20, 114

Feldman, A. 114
Ford Teaching Project 20
Foskett, N. 21, 23
Freebody, P. 115
Frost, P. 5
funded research projects 10, 24–5, 32, 39,
    59, 79–81
Furlong, J. 24

Garde-Hansen, J. 102
General Teaching Council for Wales
    (GTCW) 5, 24, 28, 39, 81
Gibbs, G. 87
Gillham, B. 66, 115
Gorard, S. 21

Governornet 59
Gregory, I. 114

Halsall, R. 23
Hargreaves, D. 21–2, 24
Hart, C. 33–4, 115
Hartley, J. 101
Healey, M. 102
Hedberg, P.R. 2, 16
Hostetler, K. 114
Hillage, J. 21
Hopkins, D. 5, 12, 20, 52, 57, 66, 85,
    114–15
Hughes, M. 2
Hughes, P. 8, 56, 101, 104, 114–15

initial teacher education and training
    (ITET) 18
Intute: Education and Research
    Methods 34

James, N. 115
James, R. 25
Jenkins, A. 102
Judge, B. 1

Karlin, N.J. 106
Kiley, M. 98
Kuit, J.A. 17

Leshem, S. 10
Lewin, K. 8
literature
    review 34–5, 39–40, 85, 119
    search 33–4, 59, 61–2, 119
Loughran, J.J. 16

McGill, I. 61
Macintyre, C. 32, 56, 66, 72, 77, 85,
    114–15
MacNaughton, G. 8, 56, 101, 104, 114–15
McNiff, J. 13, 16, 56, 114
Main, A. 2
Matthiesen, J. 10
Maxwell, J.A. 56, 115

Mertler, C.A. 8, 32, 34–5, 57, 101, 114–15
Moon, J. 1, 115
Moore, S. 101
Moseley, D. 88
Mullins, G. 98
Murray, R. 101, 105
Mutch, A. 87

negative case analysis 55
Neville, C. 85
Norris, R. 88
Norton, L.S. 8–9, 105, 114

O'Hear, A. 18
Oliver, P. 114
Oxford Learning Institute 87

Patrick, K.F. 115
Phillips, E.M. 10
Pitts, S.E. 87
Pollard, A. 2, 17
Prestage, S. 24
professional practice 11, 118
Pugh, D.S. 10

Radford, M. 21
Rae, A.M. 87
recommended further reading 1, 113–15
reflection 2, 16
reflective practice 2, 16–17, 118–19
reflective practitioners 28, 118
reflective teaching 17
reflective thinking 2, 118–19
reflective thinking exercises 2, 6, 20, 23, 29,
    32, 34, 36, 41, 47, 57, 66, 68, 73–4,
    86, 90, 93, 99, 111
reliability 54, 56, 65
research
    case study 66, 115
    classroom-based 10
    data-driven 18–19
    findings 22
    fixed-design 55
    flexible-design 55
    hypothesis 57, 68

research (*Cont'd*)
  methodology 18, 42
  methodology courses/seminars 2, 37–40
  nature of 3–5
  qualitative 45, 52–3, 55, 115
  quantitative 45, 52–3, 55, 115
  question 57
  theory-driven 18–19
research data
  analysing 1, 28, 31, 40, 66–77, 85,
    115, 119
  collecting 1–2, 28, 31, 40, 43, 45, 55–6,
    58–63, 68, 72, 85, 115, 119
    audiotape recording 55, 63,
      76, 115
    diaries 11, 55, 115
    field notes 55, 61, 115
    interview 55, 59, 72–3, 115
    observation 56, 59, 61, 115
    questionnaire 55, 59, 68–72, 115
    videotape recording 55, 63, 76, 115
  presenting 2, 77
    bar graph 77
    observation chart 59, 61, 74–5, 77,
    pie-chart 77
  qualitative 72
  quantitative 68, 72
researcher
  as performing artist 19
  as technician 19
  bias 54–5
Riehl, C. 22
Ritchie, R. 8
Robson, C. 4, 10, 20, 54–6, 114–15
Rose, R. 21–2, 24
Rumsey, S. 33, 115

Salisbury, J. 24
Schoenfeld, A.H. 22
Schön, D.A. 16
school improvement 15, 23, 28, 118

Schools Council Humanities Curriculum
    Project 20
Simons, H. 115
Slavin, R.E. 22
Somekh, B. 114
Southern Cross University 114
Stenhouse, L. 20–1

Taggart, G.L. 2
teacher
  as reflective practitioner 16–17
  as researcher 20
  research 23
  research movement 20
Teacher Research Scholarship
    scheme 24–5, 39, 81
  evaluation of 25–8
Teacher Training Resource Bank 34
Teachers' TV 115
teaching
  and learning interface 19
  as a research-based profession 21, 118
Themessl-Huber, M. 8, 114
thinking skills 25, 62–3, 76
Thomas, G. 52–3, 114–15
traditional research design 52, 55
triangulation 55
Tooley, J. 21
Trafford, V. 10
tutor-researcher relationship 19, 31, 35–6,
    42, 86, 118

validity 54–6

Wellington, J. 10, 102, 105
Whitehead, J. 13, 16, 56, 114
Wilson, A.P. 2
Wragg, E.C. 32, 52–3, 77, 115

Yin, R.K. 115
York-Barr, J. 17